WITHDRAWN

THE CREDO SERIES

VOLUMES ALREADY PUBLISHED

 # THE CREDO SERIES

PLANNED AND EDITED BY
RUTH NANDA ANSHEN

THE REDEMPTION
OF THE ROBOT

My Encounter with
Education Through Art

BY

HERBERT READ

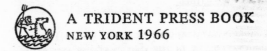

A TRIDENT PRESS BOOK
NEW YORK 1966

Prepared under the supervision of
POCKET BOOKS, INC.

LIBRARY OF CONGRESS CATALOG CARD NUMBER: 66-13041
PUBLISHED SIMULTANEOUSLY IN THE UNITED STATES AND CANADA
BY TRIDENT PRESS
MANUFACTURED IN THE UNITED STATES OF AMERICA

CONTENTS

THE CREDO SERIES

Its Meaning and Function

The Credo Series suggests that an epoch has come to an end, an epoch in which our best knowledge has been dimmed with boredom or darkened by destruction. We have felt for too long that this must be the very nature of life; this is the way life is, and to such a degree that life has consented to shrink from its own terrors, leading us to a deep apostasy of the heart and a crucifixion of our natural aspiration for experience and growth.

The absolute has surrendered to the relative. Our era of relativity, however, whether in science or in morals, does not allow us to assume that relativity implies an absence of ground to stand on, and therefore a relaxation of all effort toward foundations. "There is no firm ground," the dominant malaise of our time, this acceptance of nonfinality, summons us to a heightened task. For the failure of formulated absolutes leaves the absolute requirement to evaluate again that uncaptured reality which contains and guides the total meaning of our existence.

The Credo Series hopes to unlock a consciousness that at first sight may seem to be remote but is proved on acquaintance to be surprisingly immediate since it shows the need to reconcile the life of action with the life of contemplation, practice with principle, thought with feeling, knowledge with being, and work, no longer a form of punishment as in the Judaeo-Christian tradition but accepted as a way toward the growth and realization of the self in all its plenitude. For the whole meaning of self lies within the observer and its shadow is cast naturally on the object observed. The fragmentation of man from his work, the being of man into an eternal and temporal half, results in an estrangement of man from his creative source, from his fellows and from himself.

The symbol of *The Credo Series* is the Eye of Osiris. It is the inner Eye. Man sees in two ways: with his physical eyes, in an empirical sensing or *seeing* by direct observation, and also by an indirect envisaging. He possesses in addition to his two sensing eyes a single, image-making, spiritual and intellectual Eye. And it is the *in-sight* of this inner Eye that purifies and makes sacred our understanding of the nature of things; for that which was shut fast has been opened by the command of the inner Eye. And we become aware that to believe is to see.

Thus, it is suggested, there may be born a sharpened

vision, which comes from seeing reality as the incarnation of associations and affinities with something beyond the visible self. For it is our hope to show the human relevance of ideas, the ways in which knowledge can help us to live in the immediate and real world by pointing to the confluence of man and his vocation, of subject and object, by reverencing the curious and mysterious metabolism between man and matter, the sacred nexus between the person and his work, and by asking whether the freedom now released through the creative energies of mankind will bring salvation or destruction, the answer to which will depend upon the aims we cherish.

The Credo Series submits that the universe itself is a vast entity where man will be lost if it does not converge in the person; for material forces or energies, or impersonal ideals, or scientifically objectified learning are meaningless without their relevance for human life and their power to disclose, even in the dark tendencies of man's nature, a law transcending man's arbitrariness.

For the personal is a far higher category than the abstract universal. Personality itself is an emotional, not an intellectual, experience, and the greatest achievement of knowledge is to combine the personal within a larger unity, just as in the higher stages of development the parts that make up the whole acquire greater and greater independence and individuality within the context of the whole. Reality itself is the harmony which gives to the component particulars of a thing the equilibrium of the whole. And while physical observations are ordered with direct reference to the experimental conditions, we have in sensate experience to do with separate observations whose correlation can only be indicated by their belonging to the wholeness of mind.

It is our endeavor to show that man has reached a turning point in consciousness, that his relationship with his creative self demands a clarification that can widen and deepen his understanding of the nature of reality. Work is made for man, not man for work. This Series hopes to demonstrate the sacramental character of work which is more easily achieved when the principal objects of our attention have taken on a symbolic form that is generally recognized and accepted: in other words, when there is an established iconography relating to the meaningful interpretation of man and his vocation. This suggests a "law" in the relationship of a person and his chosen discipline: that it is valuable only when the spiritual, the creative, life is strong enough to insist on some expression through symbols. For no work can be based on material, technological or physical aspirations alone.

The human race is now entering upon a new phase of evolutionary progress, a phase in which, impelled by the forces of evolution itself, it must converge upon itself and convert itself into one single human organism dominated by a reconciliation of knowing and being in their inner unity and destined to make a qualitative leap into a higher form of consciousness that would transcend and complement individual consciousness as we know it, or otherwise destroy itself. For the entire universe is one vast field, potential for incarnation, and achieving incandescence here and there of reason and spirit. What to some is mystery and inscrutability, to others symbolizes and declares the very nature of the cosmic process. And in the whole world of *quality* with which category by the nature of our minds we necessarily make contact, we here and there apprehend pre-eminent value. This can be achieved only if we recognize that we are unable to focus our attention on the particulars of a whole without diminishing our comprehension of the whole, and of course conversely, we can focus on the whole only by diminishing our comprehension of the particulars which constitute the whole.

This Series is designed to present a kind of intellectual autobiography of each author, to portray the nature and meaning of the creative process for the creator and to show the relevance of his work to the feelings and aspirations of the man of flesh and bone. This Series endeavors to reflect also the influence of the work on the man and on society and to point to the freedom, or lack of freedom, to choose and pursue one profession rather than another. It attempts to emphasize that the creator in any realm must surrender himself to a passionate pursuit of the hidden meaning of his labors, guided by deep personal intimations of an as yet undiscovered reality.

These volumes endeavor to indicate that it is impossible to know what constitutes a good society unless we know what defines a good individual. The self is determined by the values according to which it subordinates and integrates the rest of its values. If the values be transient, so is the self. If the values be dispersed and incoherent, so is the self. If they are organic and integrated, so is the self. The unity of human personality is its soundness. The unified self cannot be understood in terms of its constituent parts as dissected away from each other. So that finally what we see and what we do are no more and no less than what we are.

It is the effort of *The Credo Series* to define the new reality in which the estrangement of man and his work, resulting in the self-estrangement in man's existence, is overcome. This new reality is born through the reconciliation of what a man *knows* with what a man *is*. Being itself in all its presuppositions and implications can only be understood through the totality, through wholeness. St. Paul, who, like Isaiah before him, went into the market place not to secularize truth but to proclaim it, taught man that the "new creation" could be explained only by conquering the daemonic cleavages, the destructive split, in soul and cosmos. And that fragmentation always destroys a unity, produces a tearing away from the source and thereby creates disunity and isolation. The fruit can never be separated from the tree. The Tree of Life can never be disjoined from the Tree of Knowledge for both have *one and the same* root. And if man allows himself to fall into isolation, if he seeks to maintain a self segregated from the totality of which he is a necessary part, if he chooses to remain asunder, unrelated to the original context of all created things in which he too has his place—including his own labors—then this act of apostasy bears fruit in the demiurgical presumption of *magic,* a form of animism in which man seeks an authority of the self, placing himself above the law of the universe by attempting to separate the inseparable. He thus creates an unreal world of false contexts after having destroyed or deserted the real. And in this way the method of analysis, of scientific objectivity, which is good and necessary in its right place, is endowed with a destructive power when it is allowed to usurp a place for which it is not fitted.

The naturalist principle that man is the measure of all things has been shattered more than ever in our own age by the question, "What is the measure of man?" Post-modern man is more profoundly perplexed about the nature of man than his ancestors were. He is on the verge of spiritual and moral insanity. He does not know who he is. And having lost the sense of who and what he is, he fails to grasp the meaning of his fellow man, of his vocation and of the nature and purpose of knowledge itself. For what is not understood cannot be known. And it is this cognitive faculty which is frequently abrogated by the "scientific" theory of knowledge, a theory that refuses to recognize the existence of comprehensive entities as distinct from their particulars. The central act of knowing is indeed that form of comprehension which is never absent from any process of knowing and is finally its ultimate sanction.

Science itself acknowledges as real a host of entities that cannot be described completely in materialistic or mechanistic terms, and it is this transcendence out of the domain of science into a region from which science itself can be appraised that *The Credo Series* hopes to expose. For the essence of the ebb and flow of experience, of sensations, the richness of the immediacy of directly apprehended knowledge, the metaphysical substance of what assails our being, is the very act itself of sensation and affection and therefore must escape the net of rational analysis, yet is intimately related to every cognitive act. It is this increasing intellectual climate that is calling into birth once more the compelling Socratic questions, "What is the purpose of life, the meaning of work?" "What is man?" Plato himself could give us only an indirect answer: "Man is declared to be that creature who is constantly in search of himself, a creature who at every moment of his existence must examine and scrutinize the conditions of his existence. He is a being in search of meaning."

Theory and life always go together. An organic conception of man and his work, man and society, man and the universe, is portrayed in First Corinthians 12 when Paul relates the famous story of the strife that once broke out between the parts of the human body. They refused to fulfill their special functions within the organism until they finally learned that they are all parts of one body and can exist and function only as such. For they all breathe together. And by so doing subordinate themselves to the presentation of the whole body. What may be an explanation of organic life in the human body may be transferred to the life in the universe and to the relationship between the interior and the exterior, for all is permeated by the life-giving creative power—by unity.

The authors in this endeavor are aware that man in the twentieth century finds himself in the greatest revolution since the discovery of agriculture. They show, each in his own way, that part of the meaning of our present turmoil may indeed lie in its being the means to reconcile thought and action, to overcome the parochialism of dogmas that only isolate man from man and man from the implicit meaning of his chosen profession. Our effort is to create an image of man intelligible and unitary, a microcosmic mirror of the greater macrocosm of which he is a part and in which he has his legitimate place in relation to the whole. For even the extraordinary successes of scientific predictions, the fruits of man's ingenuity in inventing the scientific method, seem comprehensible only on the basis that the human mind possesses an inherent logic closely parallel with the structure of the external world itself.

The very interdependence of the observer and the participant can no longer be ignored as part of the essential value of things. To take a definitive example from modern cosmology, it is challenging indeed to note that there is a most unusual connection between the existence of stars and the laws that govern the atomic nuclei. Emphasis is placed upon the existence, not the properties, of stars. For everyone expects the properties of stars and atomic nuclei to be related. It is the *connection* with the *existence* of stars that is so reassuring—and indeed surprising.

From this it is evident that there is present in the universe a *law* applicable to all nature including man and his work. Life itself then is seen to be a creative process elaborating and maintaining *order* out of the randomness of matter, endlessly generating new and unexpected structures and properties by building up associations that qualitatively transcend their constituent parts. This is not to diminish the importance of "scientific objectivity." It is, however, to say that the mind possesses a quality that cannot be isolated or known exclusively in the sense of objective knowledge. For it consists in that elusive humanity in us, our self, that knows. It is that inarticulate awareness that includes and *comprehends* all we know. It consists in the irreducible active voice of man and is recognized only in other things, only when the circle of consciousness closes around its universe of events.

The experience of the modern mind has been expressed in terms of conflict produced by false dualisms, disruption, self-destruction, meaninglessness, purposelessness and desperation. This character of our time has found its expression in literature, in art, in existential philosophy, in some forms of natural science, in political demonologies, and is explored in the psychology of the unconscious. Our authors hope to indicate that through a quickening of awareness man can overcome this dualism and can rise to face the meaning of life and work, keeping his mind and energies awake at full stretch. Such knowledge—that form of knowledge which cannot be disjoined from being—will enable man to embrace life with passion and to work with devotion. It will enable him to absorb experience with his whole nature and thereby to fill a want that is satisfied neither by action alone nor by thought alone. This unity of *being* and *doing* has a justifiable claim to be called a form of enchantment since through it men, who might otherwise give in to the malice of circumstances and conditions, find their old powers revived or new powers stirring within them, and through these life is sustained, renewed and fulfilled.

Man is now confronting himself with the compelling need to create an organic identification between what he *is* and what he *does*. For only in this way can the threat of conformism and the treachery of abstraction, the plight of the modern mind, be conquered. This split, inherited from the seventeenth century, between the transitive and the intransitive, between the creator and the process of creativity, has blunted man's appetite for experience. Language itself in our time has failed because man has forgotten that it is the mother of thought, because of its analytical emphasis, and thus lacks ready means to convey associations, emotional or imaginative, that cluster around a subject and give to it a distinctive personal significance. In other words, the symbols by which man lives and has his being, that "tacit coefficient"* of articulate knowledge that is unanalyzable, now knocks at the portals of consciousness waiting to be admitted. For human nature loses its most precious quality when it is robbed of its sense of things beyond, unexplored and yet insistent.

The Credo Series belongs to those ideas that are intuitively conceived and that originate in spheres of a spiritual order and surprise thought, as it were, compelling it to transform its inherited notions conformably with its enlarged vision of the nature of things. It

---

* See the classical work, *Personal Knowledge,* by Michael Polanyi for an enlarged meaning of the nature of reality. (Chicago University Press, 1958.)

is as though the authors of the Series were recovering this reality out of a memory of a lost harmony, a memory latent in the soul and not distilled from the changing things of mere physical observation. In this way the inner unity of the known and the knower may be preserved, and the almost mythic intuition of reality thereby related to its conceptual and rational forms of expression. For man, unlike a machine, is an organism existing as an end in itself. He *is* the system on which causal explanations are based and to which they have to return; he *is* a historically existent whole, a four-dimensional entity, and not merely an abstraction from which statements about phenomena are deducible under the guise of eternity.

Our hope is to point to a new dimension of morality —not that of constraint and prohibition but a morality that lies as a fountainhead within the human soul, a morality of aspiration to spiritual experience. It suggests that necessity is laid upon us to infer entities that are not observed and are not observable. For an unseen universe is necessary to explain the seen. The flux is seen, but to account for its structure and its nature we infer particles of various kinds to serve as the vertices of the changing patterns, placing less emphasis on the isolated units and more on the structure and nature of relations. The process of knowing involves an immaterial becoming, an immaterial identification, and finally, knowledge itself is seen to be a dependent variable of immateriality. And somewhere

along this spiritual pilgrimage man's pure observation
is relinquished and gives way to the deeper experience
of awe, for there can be no explanation of a phenomenon by searching for its origin but only by dis-
cerning its immanent law—this quality of transcendence that abides even in matter itself.

The present situation in the world and the vast ac-
cretion of knowledge have produced a serious anxiety,
which may be overcome by re-evaluating the character,
kinship, logic and operation of man in relation to his
work. For work implies goals and intimately affects
the person performing the work. Therefore the correlation and relatedness of ideas, facts and values that
are in perpetual interplay could emerge from these
volumes as they point to the inner synthesis and organic unity of man and his labors. For though no
labor alone can enrich the person, no enrichment can
be achieved without absorbing and intense labor. We
then experience a unity of faith, labor and grace
which prepares the mind for receiving a truth from
sources over which it has no control. This is especially true since the great challenge of our age arises
out of man's inventions in relation to his life.

Thus *The Credo Series* seeks to encourage the perfection not only of man's works but also and above
all the fulfillment of himself as a person. And so we
now are summoned to consider not only man in the
process of development as a human subject but also
his influence on the object of his investigation and

creation. Observation alone is interference. The naïve view that we can observe any system and predict its behavior without altering it by the very act of observation was an unjustified extrapolation from Newton's *Celestial Mechanics.* We can observe the moon or even a satellite and predict its behavior without appreciably interfering with it, but we cannot do this with an amoeba, far less with a man and still less with a society of men. It is the heart of the question of the nature of work itself. If we regard our labors as a process of shaping or forming, then the fruits of our labors play the part of a mold by which we ourselves are shaped. And this means, in the preservation of the identity of the knower and the known, that cognition and generation, that is, creation, though in different spheres, are nevertheless alike.

It is hoped that the influence of such a Series may help to overcome the serious bifurcation of function and meaning and may show that the extraordinary crisis through which the world is passing can be fruitfully met by recognizing that knowledge has not been completely dehumanized and has not totally degenerated into a mere notebook over-crowded with formulas that few are able to understand or apply.

For mankind is now engaged in composing a new theme. Life refuses to be embalmed alive. Life cannot abjure life; nothing that lives is born out of nothingness. But nothing, either, can preserve its form against the ceaseless flux of being. Life never manifests itself in negative terms. And our hope lies in drawing from every category of work a conviction that non-material values can be discovered in positive, affirmative, visible things. The estrangement between the temporal and non-temporal man is coming to an end, community is inviting communion and a vision of the human condition more worthy of man is engendered, connecting ever more closely the creative mind with the currents of spiritual energy which breaks for us the bonds of habit and keeps us in touch with the permanence of being in all its plenitude through our work.

And as, long ago, the Bearers of Bread were succeeded by the Bearers of Torches, so now, in the immediacies of life, it is the image of man and his vocation that can rekindle the high passion of humanity in its quest for light. Refusing to divorce work from life or love from knowledge, it is action, it is passion that enhances our being.

We live in an expanding universe and also in the moral infinite of that other universe, the universe of man. And along the whole stretched arc of this universe we may see that extreme limit of complicity where reality seems to shape itself within the work man has chosen for his realization. Work then becomes not only a way of knowledge, it becomes even more a way of life—of life in its totality. For the last end of every maker is himself.

"And the places that have been desolate for ages

shall be built in thee: thou shalt raise up the foundations of generation and generation; and thou shalt be
called the repairer of the fences, turning the paths
into rest."*

—RUTH NANDA ANSHEN

---

* Isaiah, 58:12

THE REDEMPTION OF THE ROBOT:
My Encounter with Education Through Art

MY CREDO

This volume in *The Credo Series* constitutes my educational *beliefs,* and for this reason appropriately belongs to a credo series. It represents my life's work and is as clear and forceful as I can make it. The words of Francis Bacon have been a guiding light throughout my life: "The mind is the man, and the knowledge of the mind. A man is but what he knoweth," but only for part of my life. These words had to be completed and the thought enlarged to include Pascal's deep perception: "The heart has its own reasons which Reason does not know; a thousand things declare it," and among these are our religious and creative instincts.

I believe that the only hope of changing the world is through those processes of physical and mental training we call *education,* but education is such a conventional word, loaded with so many meanings that stray far from my real intention, that I seek in

xxvii

vain for a new word. But even if I found one, the world would be slow to adopt it. The only possibility is to redefine the old word, and by patient exposition give it a new meaning.

For twenty years now I have been busy lecturing in many countries, writing books and articles that have had a wide circulation, and all this propaganda has been directed towards a policy called "education through art," the title of my standard book on the subject. This title has also been adopted by a society of teachers and educators in Great Britain, and in 1954 we succeeded in establishing under the auspices of UNESCO an *International Society for Education Through Art*. This Society now has many branches throughout the world.

The main difficulty encountered in our exposition of this policy is due to a misunderstanding of what we mean by the word *art*—a word as ambiguous as the word education. But again one must persist in using the conventional word and trust that the challenging association of these two misunderstood words will produce some illumination in the public mind. What I have in my own mind is a complete fusion of the two concepts, so that when I speak of art I mean an educational process, a process of upbringing; and when I speak of education I mean an artistic process, a process of self-creation. As educators, we look at the process from the outside; as artists, we look at the same process from the inside; and both processes, integrated, make the complete man.

At present, everywhere in the civilized world, we educate to promote intelligence, to promote industry, to ensure progress. It is not merely a question of promoting what the psychoanalysts call "reality adaptation"; it is to the reality of a competitive and divided society that, by existing processes of education, we seek to adapt our children. The aggressive instincts have a wonderful opportunity to discharge themselves, but it is against other children, in a ruthless struggle for places, for examination results, for class promotion. We educate to classify—that is to say, to divide—and all our efforts are expended in the cultivation of distinctions.

I believe there are two principles that should determine the aims of education, and in this credo I shall try to trace the consequence of accepting these principles. The first principle I would express as: Educate with reference to things. The second as: Educate to unite, not to divide.

By education with reference to things, I mean rather more than is usually covered by the term activist education. Activist education is sometimes directed towards divisive ends: it can be just as competitive as textbook education. My two principles, therefore, should always be considered together. What a child can accomplish unaided in the control or manipulation of things is very limited; but he soon discovers, under wise guidance, that much more can be accomplished by co-operation and mutual aid.

Education with reference to things means no more than what Plato and Rousseau meant: that education should flow through the sense, the limbs and muscles, and not primarily through the faculty of abstraction. "Keep the child dependent on things only," said Rousseau.[1] "By this course of education you will have followed the order of nature. Let his unreasonable wishes meet with physical obstacles only [in our words, let his aggressive impulses work themselves out on physical obstacles only], or with the punishment which results from his own actions, lessons which will be recalled when the same circumstances occur again. It is sufficient to prevent him from wrongdoing without forbidding him to do wrong. Experience or lack of power should take the place of law." And so on, all to illustrate Rousseau's maxim that true education consists less in precept than in practice.

Though Rousseau gave the right direction to educational theory in such a maxim, he was far from working out a system which has any relevance to our present problems, which are problems of a global scale never imagined by Plato or Rousseau. Plato, whom Rousseau regarded as the greatest of educators, is more to the point because he was a sounder moralist than Rousseau. Rousseau, typical Protestant as he

[1] *Emile,* trans. Barbara Foxley (New York, 1955).

was, found the moral law within. The love of others, he said, springs from self-love, and this is the source of human justice. But Plato found that source in the physical world, in concrete things which illustrate the harmony and divine proportion of the universe. He therefore based his system of education on the study of the arts which embody these laws—music, poetry and dancing, and, at a higher stage of education, mathematics. From this point of view Rousseau's formula—keep the child dependent on things— is not active enough, is not subtle enough. That dependence must be imitative—must be rhythmical, ritualistic, interpretative. In other words, education must be through arts, through gymnastics, through creative play of all kinds; it must be under the patronage of Dionysus rather than Apollo, and it must project, into physical celebrations, into dramatic fantasies, the aggressive impulses which are latent within us all. From this point of view the phenomenon of *catharsis*, the purgation of the emotions recognized by the Greeks as taking place in their drama, takes on a clearer significance: catharsis is precisely a discharge of aggressive impulses, and particularly of the death instinct, through imaginative participation in tragic events.

I am making the apparently paradoxical suggestion that play is the prophylactic of war. That was also Plato's suggestion, in his latest and wisest work, *The Laws*. We must spend our lives, he says (VII, 803):

in making our *play* as perfect as possible . . .
It is the current fancy [and it is a fancy *still*
current] that our serious work should be done
for the sake of our play; thus it is held that war
is serious work which ought to be well discharged
for the sake of peace. But the truth is that in
war we do not find, and we shall never find,
either any real play or any real education worth
the name, and *these* are the things I count supremely serious for such creatures as ourselves.
Hence it is peace in which each of us should
spend most of his life and spend it best. What,
then, is our right course? We should pass our
lives in the playing of games—*certain* games, that
is, sacrifice, song, and dance—with the result of
ability to gain heaven's grace, and to repel and
vanquish an enemy when we have to fight him.

But that final snag remains—"when we have to
fight." If all peoples followed the advice of Plato, then
we should all gain Heaven's grace, and there would
be no fighting between us. To the indivisibility of
peace must correspond an indivisibility of education,
and even UNESCO's efforts to that end cannot succeed so long as any nations remain committed to the
theory that war is a serious work which ought to be
well discharged for the sake of peace. What is our
solution of that dilemma?

To those who are not pacifists we can say, with
Plato, that we shall not be worse off if we behave as

Plato would have us behave. Plato was not a pacifist; on the contrary, he believed in conscription and in the same military training for boys and girls alike. But military training in those days consisted of archery and horsemanship, with a certain amount of field marching and company drill. I must confess that I see no harm in training of this kind. Military training as such is not a hardship in itself: it is the motives behind it, the moral turpitude and psychological perversity that lead to it, which make it an evil to be resisted with our utmost intelligence.

War, as Rousseau pointed out long before Tolstoy took up the theme, only makes manifest events already determined by moral causes *(Emile,* Bk. IV). For this reason our main energies must be directed against the moral causes of war. Those moral causes lie within ourselves—and pacifists should not suppose for a moment that they are pure in heart in this respect. The moral regeneration of mankind can be ccomplished only by moral education, and until ral education is given priority over all other forms ducation, I see no hope for the world. I have v indicated what I mean by moral education ducation by moral precept, but education by ctice, which in effect means education by iscipline. In the chapters that follow I describe in more detail the principles this kind of education.

edo: that the perfection of art must

arise from its practice—from the discipline of tools and materials, of form and function. I believe that it is a mistake to define a world of art and set it apart from life. I believe that it is a mistake to confine the teaching of art to appreciation, for the implied attitude is too detached. I believe that art must be practiced to be appreciated, and must be taught in intimate apprenticeship. I believe that the teacher must be no less active than the pupil. For art cannot be learned by precept, by any verbal instruction. It is, properly speaking, a contagion, and passes like fire from spirit to spirit.

I

THE EDUCATION OF FREE MEN

1. WHAT IS THE PURPOSE OF EDUCATION?

"THE TRUE OBJECT OF EDUCATION," wrote William Godwin in the first sentence of his *Enquirer* (1797), "like that of every other moral process, is the generation of happiness." I know of no better definition of the aim of education, but like all definitions, it is regressive, throwing us back on the need for further definitions. What, for example, is meant by the word generation? Is it a natural process which requires only encouragement, or is it a regimen enforced by a special technique of teaching? And can happiness be defined in a way which would include the contradictory desires of any average group of men? More interesting, perhaps, than the definition itself is Godwin's parenthesis, which asserts without argument that education is a "moral process." A century and a half ago that might have been an obvious point of view, but it is a measure of our dif-

1

ferent outlook today that we would not immediately agree that morality enters into the question. The precept "Be good, and let who will be wise" would not nowadays find acceptance even in a Sunday school. Education—we do not say, but unconsciously assume—is an acquisitive process, directed to *vocation*. It is a collecting of means for a specific end, and most of the complaints about our educational system are directed against the inadequacy of such means, or the failure to specify clearly enough the ends. Efficiency, progress, success—these are the aims of a competitive system from which all moral factors are necessarily excluded. In that respect, at least, our schools reflect truly enough our social order.

Happiness is an individual affair. It is ripeness in each fruit: the full degree of maturation, of sweetness, of fertility. But the fruit hangs on a tree, and though the fruits do not all ripen at exactly the same time, or in the same degree, the health of the tree is shown by its over-all ripeness. As Godwin went on to say, man is a social being. "In society the interests of individuals are intertwisted with each other, and cannot be separated. Men should be taught to assist each other." In other words, a factor in individual happiness is mutual aid, and these two aspects of man's existence are interdependent. Education is the process of their adjustment.

All the possible words we may use to express the purpose of education—tuition, instruction, upbring-

ing, discipline, the acquisition of knowledge, the
inculcation of manners or morality—all these reduce
to two complementary processes, which we can best
describe as "individual growth" and "social initiation."
In no respect do the educational systems characteristic
of the various nations of today favor either of these
processes. Either they force individual growth into a
pattern which destroys its natural grace and vigor;
or if a free and independent person does emerge from
the process of education, it is only to find himself at
odds with a society into whose concept of normality
he does not fit.

The trouble about happiness, as Aristotle pointed
out, is that it is a platitude: to give it as the aim of
education, or of political science, seems somewhat
superficial, especially to people with pretensions to
wisdom, who are often animated by a desire to make
men suffer before they enjoy. In Christian philosophy,
especially, there is always a premium attached to happiness. It is very necessary, of course, to deepen the
concept of happiness, because we all soon discover
how impermanent is the sense of well-being which
comes from good nourishment, a pleasant environment, adequate means and perfect health. Happiness, in a word, is *psychological,* and all material
riches are worthless unless we have peace of mind.
This was realized by the ancient philosophers, by Con-
fucius and Lâo-tse, by Socrates and Aristotle; and
they therefore defined happiness in some such words

as did Aristotle, who said that it is "an activity of the soul in accordance with perfect virtue." But that, again, is merely a definition which demands further definitions, and so Aristotle had to define what he meant by *virtue*. He came to the conclusion that there was no such thing as virtue, but only virtues, intellectual and moral. Wisdom and understanding, knowing how to act or behave in given circumstances, the science of life—that is one aspect of virtue; but a man may have all this knowledge but not be able to control his own impulses and desires. He may have perfect understanding, but be a creature of bad habits. Knowledge and self-discipline are therefore two different aspects of virtue, both essential to happiness and both to be learned in the normal course of education.

The difference between these two aspects of virtue —let us follow the usual practice and call them intellectual and moral virtue—is that whilst the first can be made a subject of general agreement, the second depends on the temperament or disposition of the individual. Intellectual virtue can be codified and accepted as a system of beliefs and customs; but moral virtue is the interior function of each man's physiological and nervous make-up. Since a man deficient in moral virtue cannot be expected to appreciate properly the values of intellectual virtue, moral virtue has a fundamental priority in education. The first question in education, therefore, is how best to develop the moral virtues of children—that is to say, how best to train the physical senses with which each individual is endowed so that they mature to that state of temperance, harmony and skill which will enable the individual to pursue the intellectual virtues in freedom of will and singleness of mind.

Aristotle pointed out that moral virtue—the integrated personality, as modern psychologists would say—comes about as a result of habit. We are conditioned by nature to form habits, and the form our habits should take is inherent in nature. "Neither by nature, then, nor contrary to nature do the virtues arise in us; rather we are adapted by nature to receive them and are made perfect by habit."

The pattern of those habits which we are adapted to receive—i.e., to be taught—is found in nature: from nature we must take that pattern, and by habituating our children to that pattern, we shall perfect their moral virtue and enable them to achieve true happiness. That does not mean that we are slaves to nature, but that we can discover freedom only in nature. The free man is a man of nature, perfected in natural ways of behaviour.

Such is the theory of Aristotle: he derived it in a large measure from Plato, and to Plato we must turn for a detailed account of this natural pattern and of the only effective method of adapting ourselves to it. But first let us note that the general tradition of education in Europe and America since the Renaissance has neglected or distorted this classical theory of education—first by blurring the clear distinction between intellectual and moral virtue, and then by ignoring the essential priority of moral virtue, by attempting to inculcate intellectual virtue into minds which have not received the necessary preparation. It is only onto a stock of goodness that knowledge can be safely grafted: by grafting it onto stocks that are unbalanced, undeveloped, neurotic, we merely give power to impulses that may in themselves be evil or corrupted.

2. THE PATTERN IN NATURE

To suggest that the pattern of moral virtue is to be found in nature seems immediately to involve us in a scientific approach to our subject. We have become so prejudiced by the claims put forward by certain scientists that we have been content to leave "nature" to science, and to let it be assumed that "art" is something outside nature. Science implies measurement and classification—what is called "scientific method" or analysis. But it is only one "method," and wisdom, which includes science in its scope, implies also synthesis—the apprehension and understanding of wholes and relationships, the workings of the imagination and creative activity—in short, a subjective and sensational approach to reality; and this aspect of wisdom might be called the method of art, or the "aesthetic method." As such, it must be regarded as an indispensable instrument of education; and since the scientific method is not within the mental capacity of young children, and the aesthetic method is natural to them, we must turn to art as the only method available for the first stages of education.

During the present century a world-wide revolution has taken place in the appreciation of children's art; gradually we have come to realize that we have in art an instrument of education and not merely a subject to be taught. Children have an art, that is to say, a way of expressing themselves in visual and plastic images, appropriate to their stage of mental development, and this pictorial language of theirs is something which exists in its own right and which is not to be judged by adult standards. It is a means of communication possessed by every child, and one that can be used to give us an understanding of the child and to give the child an understanding of its environment. Art is not now an "extra": we no longer seek to pick out a few children with what used to be called an artistic temperament, and educate this minority to be artists. We recognize an artist of some kind in every child, and we maintain that the encouragement of a normal creative activity is one of the essentials of a full and balanced development of the personality.

This is a revolution to which many philosophers,

psychologists and teachers have contributed, but it was John Ruskin who first suggested that the child's artistic activity should be entirely voluntary. It was an English psychologist, James Sully, who first made any considerable study of the characteristics of this voluntary activity. But great educationalists all over the world, following the lead of Froebel, were beginning to insist on the importance of spontaneity in all forms of education. The position we have now reached implies a claim that of all forms of spontaneous activity, a special educative value attaches to the artistic activity.

From this point of view, art is not to be treated as something external which has to be inserted into the general scheme of education. Nor, on the other hand, can education be regarded as something which can never be complete without art. There is a certain way of life which we hold to be good, and the creative activity we call art is essential to it. Education is nothing but an initiation into this way of life, and we believe that in no way is that initiation so successfully achieved as through the practice of art.

Art, that is to say, is a way of education—not so much a subject to be taught as a method of teaching any and all subjects. For this view of the educative role of art, no originality can be claimed: we are but restating in modern terms the ideals which Plato expressed twenty-four centuries ago. And when we say we are restating these ideals in modern terms we do not mean that we are adapting Plato's ideas to modern needs. We are not distorting his meaning or intention in any one particular. When Plato uses abstract terms like harmony, grace and rhythm, and when we use the same abstract terms, we want to convey exactly the same meaning. It is only when we use more particular terms, like music or painting or architecture, that we diverge a little from Plato in that we illustrate our meaning from our richer store of experience. It does not follow that we are any nearer to the truth than Plato, but we are entitled to claim, if we have any faith at all in human evolution, that the use we can make of arts like music or painting or architecture is potentially much greater than it was for Plato. But only potentially. For what is the history of the modern world, a world so rich potentially, but one long record of unrealized potentialities, of missed opportunities? Not much is known about that obscure subject, Greek music; but not even our classical scholars have ventured to suggest that Greek music was anything but a primitive affair in comparison with the music of Bach, of Mozart, of Beethoven. But what proportional use have we ever made of this modern art in education? Our music, compared with Greek music, is a veritable extension of human sensibility. But what commensurate place does it occupy in our schools? We have eurhythmics, it is true, and let us pay all honor to Dalcroze, who has in this one aspect of education set us on the right path. But even in those schools which have been wholly devoted to Dalcroze's ideals, it is to be doubted whether we have advanced even so far as the educational methods contemplated by Plato on the basis of the primitive music of Greece.

The claims made by Plato for an aesthetic mode of education are quite simply stated. Indeed, one cannot do better than translate Plato's own words. "We attach such supreme importance to musical education" —he makes Socrates say in the *Republic* (III, 401-2) —"because rhythm and harmony sink most deeply into the recesses of the soul, and take most powerful hold of it, bringing gracefulness in their train, and making a man graceful if he be rightly nurtured, but if not, the reverse." Plato then describes, in what we call considerable psychological detail, the exact effects of rhythm and harmony on the growing mind. But he does not, as is too often assumed in the discussions of his educational theories, ascribe these qualities to music only. He says that the same qualities "enter largely into painting and all similar workmanship, into weaving and embroidery, into architecture, as well as the whole manufacture of utensils in general, nay, into the constitution of living bodies, and of all plants; for in all these things gracefulness or ungracefulness finds place." And he adds, for he has always the negative picture in mind, "The absence of grace, rhythm, and harmony is closely related to an evil style and an evil character."

There is something at once so simple and so comprehensive about this theory of Plato's that really we do not need to go beyond it. Music, painting, the making of useful objects, the proportions of the living body and of plants, these will, if made the basis of our educational methods, instill into the child a grace and harmony which will give it, not merely a noble bearing, but also a noble character; not only a graceful body, but also a sober mind. It will do this, says Plato, long before the child is able to reason, because it will inculcate what he calls, "the instinct of relationship,"[1] and it is upon this instinct that reason itself depends. Possessing this instinct, the child will never do wrong in deed or in thought.

I ought perhaps to explain at this point what Plato meant by this "instinct of relationship," for it is the foundation of his theory of education, and one, moreover, which he never abandoned throughout the development of this thought. The theory as I have already given it comes from the *Republic*. This was a work of the philosopher's early maturity. Thirty years later, at the age of seventy, Plato wrote his *Laws*, which the late Professor A. E. Taylor, one of the greatest of modern Platonists, has described as "today the least generally known of Plato's major compositions," and yet "in some respects his most

---

[1] This is, of course, a translator's phrase (Davies and Vaughan) and not always adopted by other translators. But it represents accurately enough Plato's general meaning.

characteristic work."[2] Here, in Book II, we find his theory of education through art restated in unmistakable terms—"handled," as Professor Taylor says, "with a psychological thoroughness to which the *Republic* affords no parallel." The theory, I would maintain, is as simple as it is true. It is this: that the aim of education should be to associate feelings of pleasure with what is good and feelings of pain with what is evil. Now such *feelings* are aesthetic—a fact which would have been obvious to the Greeks. This word aesthetic as we use it is cold and abstract, but it indicates a relationship which to the Greeks was very real and organic, a property of the physiological reactions which take place in the process of perception.

Now, says Plato, there exist in the physical universe, which we experience through our senses, certain rhythms, melodies, and abstract proportions which when perceived convey to the open mind a sensation of pleasure. For the moment we need not consider *why* these rhythms and proportions exist: they are simply part of the given universe. But if, says Plato, we can associate the concrete sensation of pleasure given by these rhythms and proportions with good, and the concrete sensation of pain given by the opposite qualities of disharmony and ugliness with evil; if we can do this systematically in the early years, while the infant mind is still open to such influences,

---

[2] *The Laws of Plato*, trans. A. E. Taylor (London, 1934).

then we shall have set up an association between natural and spontaneous feelings and graceful or noble behaviour. Lest it should be thought that I am reading into Plato more than is justified, let me quote his actual words, as translated by Professor Taylor:

And therefore what I would say is this: a child's first infant consciousness is that of pleasure and pain, this is the domain wherein the soul first acquires virtue or vice. . . . By education I mean goodness in the form in which it is first acquired by a child. In fact, if pleasure and liking, pain and dislike, are formed in the soul on right lines before the age of understanding is reached, and when that age is attained, these feelings are in concord with understanding, thanks to early discipline in appropriate habits—this concord, regarded as a whole, is virtue. But if you consider the one factor in it, the rightly disciplined state of pleasures and pains whereby a man, from his first beginnings on, will abhor what he should abhor and relish what he should relish—if you isolate this factor and call it education, you will be giving it its true name.

Plato then illustrates his argument in this way:

No young creature whatsoever . . . can keep its body or its voice still: they are all perpetually trying to make movements and noises. They leap and bound, they dance and frolic, as it were with glee, and again, they utter cries of all sorts. Now animals at large have no perception of order or disorder in these motions, no sense of what we call rhythm or melody.

But man, Plato goes on to point out, is distinguished from the rest of animal creation precisely by the fact that he possesses an aesthetic sense, which he defines as "the power to perceive and enjoy rhythm and melody." Link this power of aesthetic perception to the power of discriminating between good and evil and then the most fundamental aim of education has been achieved. Good is *spontaneously* associated with pleasure, evil with pain.

Such is Plato's theory of education, and it seems to be essentially simple and obviously true. Why, then, should it offer such difficulty and, indeed, incomprehensibility to the modern educator? Professor Taylor, in his Introduction to his translation of the *Laws*, offers this explanation:

To Plato, as a true Greek, the ugliness of conduct which is morally out of place is the most immediately salient fact about it, and the beauty of holiness, if the scriptural phrase may be permitted, is something more than a metaphor. To judge by the tone of much of our literature, we are less sensitive on the point; we seem slow to perceive ugliness in wrong-doing as such, or even

ready to concede the 'artistry' of great wicked-
ness. It may be a wholesome discipline to consider carefully whether this difference of feeling
may not be due less to a confusion on Plato's
part between the beautiful and the morally good
than to a certain aesthetic imperceptiveness on
ours.

3. ART AND HUMAN NATURE

Plato was an authoritarian. His political utopia has
always been a model for exponents of the totalitarian
state. It is therefore necessary to ask ourselves whether
there does not lurk in this theory of education some
denial of that freedom and integrity of the human
personality which is the basis of our libertarian philosophy. Granted the prevalence of "aesthetic imperceptiveness," this danger would surely exist: the "order
of nature" would be interpreted in a systematic and
insensitive manner, and the emergent faculties of the
child would then be "conditioned" to this rigid pattern. Plato's republic can undoubtedly be regarded
as a rigid pattern of this kind: it is the creation of a
poet, but its beauty is objective, calculated, classical:
it is like a crystal of ice. But nature is a living growth,
and human nature is warm and mobile. Between
the form natural to growth, which is a creative
achievement of the life force or whatever impulse
animates organic matter, and the forms abstracted

by the human intellect, there is this difference: the one is a continuing process of freedom or spontaneity, of growth and integration, whereas the other is an act of objectification, or externalization and fixation, of cooling and petrification. Our criticism of Plato, if this were the place to pursue it, would charge him with abstracting from the natural process, making of it a measured pattern, and thereby destroying its quality of spontaneity, which in the human personality is the quality of spiritual freedom.

Two quite distinct developments during the past sixty years have made it possible for us to accept Plato's theory of the place of art in education without incurring the dangers which it would offer to imperceptive minds. One is the complete revolution which has taken place in our conception of art itself, and the other is the revolution in psychology.

The revolution in art is by no means complete, nor has a definite new standard or style yet been established. To some people it seems that the present state of art is merely confused and incoherent. But it must be obvious, even to the most bewildered spectator of the modern scene, that there is more essential similarity between a modern functional building and the Parthenon than between the Parthenon and the classical buildings of our own time. The functional building and the Parthenon both exhibit the same fundamental features of good architecture—fitness for purpose, harmony of proportions, good manners—

whereas a modern building in the classical style can be described only as a fantasy in architectural inappropriateness. As for modern painting, there again one need not accept all its confused manifestations as a progress towards the ideal of beauty which Plato had in mind. Nevertheless, those with an eye to see, and no censoring prejudice, will find among these confused manifestations of the modern spirit works of art which answer to the Platonic canon, and are symbols of the grace and rhythm and harmony which led Plato to make art the basis of his educational system. One can assert of all the arts that a spirit of enquiry and scientific understanding has, during the last thirty years or so, led us back to the basic principles, and that though we cannot yet point to the creative achievements of a great age, we are now in a position to understand the significance of art such as has not existed since Plato's time. That is a large claim to make for the modern philosophy of art; it is perhaps a conceited claim. But however humble and soberminded we may be, it is difficult to find any intermediate period which reached such an understanding. It is true that during the Renaissance there were great humanists like Alberti who owed much to the Platonic doctrine, and the art of that period was, of course, a much nearer approximation to Plato's ideals than anything we have so far produced in the modern period. But neither Alberti nor any of the later humanists, however far they went in the direction of identifying moral and aesthetic ideals, ever committed themselves to anything as radical as an aesthetic method of education. They were all grammarians at heart, and like Browning's hero (of "The Grammarian's Funeral"), had "decided not to live but know," a noble ideal for the few who are content to work "dead from the waist down," but not a principle for those who believe with Plato that the function of education is to promote the good life.

However much an increased understanding of the nature of art has enabled us to appreciate the truth and relevance of Plato's theory of education, we have been helped in an even larger measure by the increased understanding of human nature which we owe to modern psychology. To demonstrate this fact adequately would lead us into a technical discussion which would not be appropriate now, but perhaps I might briefly indicate three directions in which modern psychology tends to support our claims.

The first relates to the significance of imagery in thought—imagery of all kinds, although it is simpler to discuss the subject in terms of visual imagery. We know, on the basis of many recent experiments, that the child begins life with a mind full of extremely vivid imagery. One school of psychologists even maintains that in the first years the child has difficulty in distinguishing between its perceptions of the external world and its secondary images, and that the normal memory-image is only gradually separated from these vivid eidetic images. Whatever may be the truth of this theory, we do know for certain that the next stage in development, the stage of conceptual thought, is reached only by the gradual suppression of imagery. Now the whole Aristotelian tradition in education is so committed to the superiority of conceptual or logical processes of thought that all means have been taken to drive images out of the child's mind and to make it an efficient thinking machine. It was accepted as axiomatic that logical methods of procedure were uniquely efficient, and the ambition of every pedagogue was to devise a logical scheme for every subject in the curriculum. It was experimentally established that images performed no useful function in abstract thought, and the more abstract the thought the more intelligent it was assumed to be. To quote a well-known British educationalist:[3]

> Those children of the most fertile imagery . . . were by no means those of the highest school intelligence . . . the correlations between vivid and clear visual and auditory imagery and school intelligence are low, or it may be negative. . . .

I have no desire to question these established facts. But what we must question is the standard of "school intelligence" implicit in all such tests. It is nothing but the logical bias in its most blatant form. We know

[3] Charles Fox, *Educational Psychology* (London, 1930), p. 86.

the examinations and tests by means of which the standard is established. Most of us have suffered from their indignities. But now, with the support of other schools of psychology, we are in a position to challenge the whole of this logical or rationalistic tradition. We must not commit the mistake of putting forward another exclusive standard. Our science teaches us toleration. But we do assert, on evidence, that there is more than one standard of intelligence, and indeed, more than one mode of thought. The purpose of thought is to arrive at truth, and truth, we say, is not found exclusively in the possession of those with a high "intelligence quotient"; it is just as likely to proceed out of the mouths of babes and sucklings, poets and artists, even madmen.

What has been established, by the particular school of psychology we are relying on, is that these babes and sucklings, poets and painters, visionaries of all kinds, have one thing in common—an imagination so vivid that it must be regarded as the use of the particular kind of imagery, that kind already referred to which has been called eidetic imagery. This imagery, which is natural to babes and sucklings, is in certain rare cases retained beyond adolescence, and among these rare cases are to be found our poets and painters and visionaries of all kinds. But more: when we come to investigate the nature of scientific thought in so far as this thought is an inventive or creative activity, and not merely a logical arrangement of accepted facts, we find that it too relies on images. The whole of modern physics, for example, is studded with imagery, from Newton's falling apple to Eddington's man in a lift. Possibly there is more imagery in modern physics than in modern poetry.

With such facts in our hands we need not stop to defend the biological utility of the arts. We can turn on the scientists and convince them on the evidence of their own processes of thought. In so far as it is creative and biologically useful, their thought is imaginative. Yet the systems of education which they have devised, and the tests which they have imposed on children, give no marks to the imagination. Images, they say *and prove,* are not essential to efficient thought. So everything is done to suppress these inconvenient sprites and to enthrone the absolute rule of the concept in the child's mind.

The second direction from which we receive psychological support for our claims is known as the Gestalt theory. It is hardly possible to express the significance of this theory in a few simple words, but the exponents of the theory would agree that it too is in the main a protest against a logical conception of knowledge and science. What they say, in effect, is that there are no facts apart from the act or process of experiencing them, that the "facts of a case" are not grasped by enumeration, but must be felt as a coherent pattern. The word "felt" must be emphasized, for this factor of feeling in perception is aesthetic. It is not only the perception of a particular pattern, but also a discrimination in favor of that particular pattern. That is to say, out of all possible patterns of behaviour, one is chosen as being particularly fit or appropriate. It feels right—one feels at once the ease with which this particular pattern is apprehended and the appropriateness of the action that ensues. And then, since this particular pattern of behaviour feels right, it tends to be repeated, and other modes of behaviour tend to become assimilated to it.

What the psychologists call the acquisition of a pattern of behaviour is nothing but the process of learning—learning, that is to say, in the sense of acquiring skill in the doing of anything—walking, skating, weaving, painting, assembling an engine. Says one of the Gestalt psychologists:

> Grace and skill go hand in hand; their achievement is never the result of combining acts which themselves are awkward and unskilful. In order to do anything gracefully and skilfully, one must first hit upon the 'fortunate variation' in behaviour which is most suitable to the conditions.

This has led us back to Plato again. In that part of the *Republic* which precedes the theory of education already referred to, Plato analyzes the nature of form and rhythm, and what he says in effect is that the laws of form and rhythm are not given *a priori*, but are to be discovered in the best and most efficient actions. The following passage is from the *Republic,* and not from the work of a modern Gestalt psychologist. In studying the law of rhythms, Plato says:

> We must not aim at a variety of them, or study all movements indiscriminately, but observe what are the natural rhythms of a well regulated and manly life, and when we have discovered these we must compel the foot and the music to suit themselves to the sense of such life, and not the sense itself to the foot and the music.

In other words, in modern words, aesthetic laws are inherent in the biological processes of life itself; they are the laws which guide life along the path of ease and efficiency; and it is our business as educationalists to discover these laws in nature or experience and make them the principles of our teaching. Balance and symmetry, proportion and rhythm, are basic factors in experience: indeed, they are the only elements by means of which experience can be organized into persisting patterns, and it is of their nature that they imply grace, economy and efficiency. What feels right works right, and the result, as measured by the consciousness of the individual, is a heightened sense of aesthetic enjoyment.

We now come to the final aspect of the psychological evidence. It is even more difficult to summarize than the last-mentioned aspect, but for a different reason. The evidence is not complete. We have indeed got out of our depths and we flounder in a stormy sea. The theory of the unconscious is still disputed, and we must be careful not to claim too high a therapeutic value for those forms of free expression which we wish to encourage as part of our educational methods. That the young child—the very young child—has its repressions and its complexes no less than its parents and teachers is now sufficiently evident, but the treatment of psychoses and neuroses in the child presents quite exceptional difficulties to the psychiatrist. It is not, of course, for the teacher to meddle in such matters without training, but the psychiatrist might well ask the teachers to co-operate with him. Apart from any other aspect of the question, a child's drawings, produced as a result of spontaneous activity, are direct evidence of the child's physiological and psychological disposition, and in the opinion of some professional psychoanalysts, these drawings have more clinical value than any other form of evidence. But that is an aspect of the matter for which we must seek expert guidance. There is, however, a simpler aspect which is well within our lay competence. We know that a child absorbed in drawing or in any other creative activity is a happy child. We know just as a matter of everyday experience that self-expression is self-improvement. For that reason we must claim a large portion of the child's time for

artistic activities, simply on the grounds that these
activities are, as it were, a safety valve, a path to
equableness. That is a practical reason which might
convince the reluctant logicians, but, of course, it is
not our main reason for claiming a large portion of
the child's time. We cannot hope to overcome
the ramparts of the rationalist tradition with our real
reason, for that would seem too impracticable, too
idealistic. For our real claim has no limits. We do
not claim an hour or a day of the child's time; we
claim the whole child. We believe that we have
within our grasp a method of education of absolutely
universal validity. We believe that the grace we can
instil by means of music, poetry and the plastic arts
is not a superficial acquirement, but the key to all
knowledge and all noble behaviour. We suspect that
much, if not all, of the misery in the world today is
due to the suppression of imagination and feeling in
the child, to the prevalence of logical and rationalistic
modes of thought that do violence to those principles
of grace and rhythm and fair proportion which are
implicit in the order of the universe. We believe that
our function, not merely as artists and art teachers,
but as teachers and exemplars in general, is, as Plato
said in one of his most visionary flights:

To be guided by our instinct for whatever is
lovely and gracious, so that our young men,
dwelling in a wholesome climate, may drink in

good from every quarter, whence, like a breeze bearing health from happy regions, some influence from noble works constantly falls upon eye and ear from childhood upward, and imperceptibly draws them into sympathy and harmony with the beauty of reason, whose impress they take.[4]

4. *THE UNIQUENESS OF THE PERSON*

These influences of which Plato speaks fall upon the organs of a unique sensibility. Uniqueness is a natural fact. It is a result of the infinite permutations and combinations of the *genes* which are the agents of life transmitted and united in the process of conception. Identical twins, by the uniqueness of their identity, give us a measure of the enormous diversity of persons in general.

This diversity is not a biological accident. It is the dialectical basis of natural selection, of human evolution. Any attempt, therefore, whether by education or coercion, to eliminate the differences between persons would frustrate the natural dissemination and growth of the human race. It is possible and even "scientific" to hold that we should attempt to control this growth, just as we have controlled the growth of species like the horse and the sheep. But such control

[4] Trans. F. S. Cornford (Oxford, 1941).

could only be effectively exercised if we had an agreed aim in view. We breed horses for strength or speed, sheep for a finer fleece. But it is a godlike assumption to breed the human race for any predetermined quality, and the idea has entered the minds of only totalitarian philosophers like Plato and Hegel, or been the policy of extreme fanatics who have attempted to put the ideals of such philosophers into practice.

Opposed to this point of view is another equally extreme—it received its extreme expression in the philosophy of Max Stirner, to which Marx and Engels devoted some of their most destructive criticism. This philosophy asserts, with a logical consistency which some of its opponents might emulate, that all values can be received and judged only through the instrumentality of a unique sensational system, and that everything exterior to the wishes and desires of this ego is either a false rationalization of these instinctive drives or a form of self-deception which leads to frustration and eventually to aggression and self-destruction. Altruism, that is to say, is an illusion, and only by recognizing that fact can we achieve individual happiness.

The truth, as it is manifested in events, lies somewhere between these two extremes. "History," wrote Engels:

> makes itself in such a way that the final result always arises from conflicts between many individ-

ual wills, of which each again has been made what it is by a host of particular conditions of life. Thus there are innumerable intersecting forces, an infinite series of parallelograms of forces which give rise to one resultant—the historical event. This again may itself be viewed as the product of a power which, taken as a whole, works *unconsciously* and without volition. For what each individual wills is obstructed by everyone else, and what emerges is something that no one willed.[5]

It is not the purpose of education to eliminate this conflict between individual wills—the attempt would be foredoomed to failure because the conflict is inherent in our biological nature. But obviously "the historical event" would be very different if, instead of a blind clash of individual wills, we could substitute some form of willing accommodation.

Two necessary processes are involved. One we shall call *initiation;* the other, *reciprocity.* Before we can give effective direction to these processes, we must give precision to the units involved. A game cannot be played to a conclusion unless the counters have a fixed value; trade cannot be carried on without specific tokens of exchange; and in the same way a society can function harmoniously only if the individuals composing it are integrated persons, that is to say, people whose physical and mental growth has been

---

[5] Tolstoy expressed a similar view of history in *War and Peace.*

completed, so that they are whole and healthy, and by that very reason competent to render mutual aid.

We shall deal with the processes of initiation and reciprocity presently: but first we must recognize the biological significance of uniqueness. It is true that we come into the world trailing clouds of glory; a Heaven which is universal and impersonal lies about us in our infancy, and though the shades of the social prison-house begin to close on the growing boy, he is still in Wordsworth's exact phrase, "nature's priest." Each infant mind is endowed with his share of a racial consciousness (an "archaic heritage," as Freud calls it). But this is but one component in a system of perceptions and instincts, a "vision splendid," that is unique. Why we affirm this uniqueness, and do not want it to "die away, and fade into the light of common day," why we do not want it to be "ironed out" by impersonal powers, is explained by our reading of the biological evidence. At the heart of life is what is sometimes called a *dialectic,* but which is quite simply a strife between positive and negative forces, between Love and Death; and it is out of the tension created by this strife that further vitality, or what is optimistically called progress, arises. We can even venture to say that the more definite the terms of this opposition—the sharper the conflict—the more vigorous will be the life. The first charge on the educator, therefore, is to bring the uniqueness of the individual into focus, to the end that a more vital interplay of forces takes place within each organic grouping of individuals—within the family, within the school, within society itself. The possibilities are at first evenly weighed between *hatred*, leading to crime, unhappiness and social antagonism, and *love*, which ensures mutual aid, individual happiness and social peace. What is certain is that the more desirable outcome is not ensured simply by the forcible suppression of the less desirable instincts: the whole meaning of education is that we seek to avoid hate by *positive* means, that is to say, by encouraging the stronger growth of love, which is indeed that grain of mustard seed "which a man took, and sowed in his field, which is indeed the greatest among herbs, and becometh a tree, so that the birds of the air come to lodge in the branches thereof."

5. THE PARENT AND THE CHILD

The first and most fundamental stage of education is carried on in the family circle. This fact, which in all its potentialities has always been realized by the Catholic Church, has only recently been given "scientific" demonstration through the practice of psychoanalysis. Only a tradition of education which for centuries has cultivated intellectual virtue at the expense of moral virtue could have ignored so vital a consideration. The exponents of that tradition, who have not usually seized on children before the age of seven or eight, have then tried, and often tried in vain, to "mould the character" of those committed to their care but the truth is that "the little human being is frequently a finished product in his fourth or fifth year, and only gradually reveals in later years what lies buried in him."[6]

It is not possible to study the implications of psychoanalysis for education without becoming convinced that they are of overwhelming importance, and that it is futile to discuss theories of education for the later stages of the child's life until we have made some reasonable provision for the first phase, during which the child is still physically dependent on its parents and largely abandoned to their care. That this care is often inspired by loving-kindness is not a sufficient guarantee of its efficiency. Children, psychologically speaking, can be killed by kindness, or "spoilt." In our present civilization we have to deal with a situation that has become a systematic hypocrisy, organized by neurotics, and into this system the child enters, not armed with powers of resistance, but doomed to conformity.

He is doomed by his impulse to imitate, or identify himself with, some adult in the family circle—usually the mother or father. The boy may wish to be as big and strong as his father, but at the same time he is in

---

[6] Freud, *Introductory Lectures on Psycho-analysis* (London, 1922), p. 298.

love (and in a very real sense) with his mother. Gradually this boy begins to feel that his father stands in his way with his mother. His identification with his father then takes on what Freud calls "a hostile colouring" and becomes identical with "the wish to replace his father in regard to his mother." The child is therefore in its earliest years caught up in a crisscross of instinctive reactions which involve love and hate even towards the same object. This naturally leads to a mental state of insecurity or anxiety, and since the basic instinct in life is to protect one's own life—to live securely and full of contentment—there is an equally natural instinct to repress those reactions of hate which we find lead to discontent and unhappiness. But psychoanalysis has shown that an instinct is never repressed without seeking unconscious compensation. We cannot, in this short treatise on a general subject, go into the details of all the psychological processes involved: it is sufficient to say that psychoanalysis finds in this universal situation of the infant a sufficient explanation of all those aggressive impulses, jealousies, tempers, bad manners and selfishness which it is the particular purpose of moral education to restrain or transform.

The educator must therefore ask, to what extent can this situation itself be dealt with, so that the development of these aggressive impulses is foreseen and controlled? To that question the psychoanalysts have given no very definite answer. Freud himself seems to deprecate analysis of normal children. "Such a prophylactic against nervous disease," he wrote, "which would probably be very effective, *presupposes an entirely different structure of society*. The application of psychoanalysis to education must be looked for today in quite a different direction." And he then goes on to give a definition of education which to some of his followers has seemed somewhat reactionary.

> Let us get a clear idea of what the primary business of education is. The child has to learn to control its instincts. To grant it complete freedom, so that it obeys all its impulses without any restriction, is impossible. . . . The function of education . . . is to inhibit, forbid and suppress, and it has at all times carried out this function to admiration. But we have learnt from analysis that it is this very suppression of instinct that involved the danger of neurotic illness. . . . Education has . . . to steer its way between the Scylla of giving the instincts free play and the Charybdis of frustrating them. Unless the problem is altogether insoluble, an optimum of education must be discoverable, which will do the most good and the least harm. It is a matter of finding out how much one may forbid, at which times *and by what methods*. And then it must be further considered that the children have very different constitutional dispositions, so that the same ed-

ucational procedure cannot possibly be good for all children.[7]

Later in this same paragraph Freud enumerates the task of the educator as: (a) to recognize the characteristic constitution of each child; (b) to guess from small indications what is going on in its unformed mind; (c) to give him the right amount of love, and at the same time (d) to preserve an effective degree of authority.

This approach to the first phase of the child's life has carried us beyond the family circle into the general field of education. But it should be obvious from this very brief consideration of the problem that the relationship first established between the child and its parents, and then extended to the family circle, is fundamental. Joined to the innate disposition of the child (its physically determined temperament), this first stage of growth and initiation controls all the later stages. If the behaviour of parents towards their children were dependent on learning a technique (as the behaviour of the teacher is held to be), the situation of mankind would be desperate. Luckily, in this respect healthy parents are guided by healthy instincts, and mutual love between parents and children can prevent and heal the wounds to which we are liable. But more often than not in the modern

[7] *New Introductory Lectures* (London, 1933), pp. 191–92. (Author's italics.)

world parents are not healthy: they participate in a vast social neurosis, which has many causes and many aspects, but which is essentially due to that drastic suppression of the sexual impulses demanded by our modern civilization. It follows from this that the reform of education can never be a departmental affair: it is the whole man that is spiritually sick, and we cannot make him well by repressing this or that aspect of his daily existence. At the same time it is too optimistic to assume that a particular social revolution will carry all the necessary reforms in its sweep. It is man's relationship to society itself that is wrong, and none of the forms of society which at present prevail or are in prospect attempts to change that relationship. Parents, family, school, workshop, local environment—all that is still a *physical* or biological reality to which the child can be emotionally and morally related; beyond are the abstractions of church, state and nation to which only the mind responds, a mind open to the ambiguity of words, symbols and ideals, the ground of all our misunderstandings, an unreal world which bears no correspondence to the pattern of nature.

6. THE TEACHER AND THE CHILD

Neither in the passage I have quoted nor elsewhere in his writings does Freud venture to suggest even the outlines of a successful *method* of education. But it will be seen that he tends to throw the burden on the individual educator: that is to say, there is no single psychologically correct system of education, but only the possibility of developing a right relationship between the particular teacher and his pupil. This is in line with the general doctrine of psychoanalysis, which is a psychology of individuals. (The psychology of the group must seek some other name, such as phyloanalysis.) The assumption is, of course, a realistic one, for however much a child may be influenced by the environment of a particular school or the general aspects of a particular discipline, the funnel through which this experience is poured into his mind is always the individual teacher. This is due, not only to the fact that it is the obvious function of the teacher to mediate between his pupil and the outer world, but even more to that process of identification to which I have already referred and which is one of the psychological mechanisms whose existence and scope have been revealed by psychoanalysis. This "earliest expression of an emotional tie with another person" (the boy with his father, for example) soon takes on complexities due to what we would normally call subjective and objective attitudes (e.g., the boy's desire to *be like* his father and the boy's desire at the same time to *have* his father). Without going into all the further complexities which ensue in the family circle, it should be obvious that a new situation arises when the child leaves the family circle for the school and finds there another adult with whom he must develop an emotional tie. The result in most cases is a transference—partial or complete—of the symptoms of identification from the parent to the teacher. Incidentally, other children are experiencing the same transference, from *different* parents to the *same* teacher, and this mutual tie is the nucleus of the first *group* in whose unity the child is likely to participate.[8] This is the situation of which the teacher has to take advantage and it is one which requires infinite tact and charity. It easily degenerates, on his part, into an attitude of dominance, and on the part of the child, into a state of hypnotic dependence. (The parallel in the wider sphere of politics will be obvious.)

During the course of this change from absolute dependence on and ideal identification with the parent, there is established in the mind of the individual what Freud has called the "super-ego." The "ideal" element is, as it were, separated from the physical parent, and becomes the growing child's conscience, his faculty of self-observation and moral purpose. Freud himself has observed that "during the course of its growth, the super-ego also takes over the influence of those

[8] Freud, *Group Psychology and Analysis of the Ego,* p. 80:
A primary group of this kind is a number of individuals who have substituted one and the same object for their ego ideal and have consequently identified themselves with one another in their ego.

persons who have taken the place of the parents, that is to say, of persons who have been concerned in the child's upbringing, and whom it has regarded as ideal models."[9] This gives the teacher his only possibility for what is called "character-formation." Unfortunately, as Freud also pointed out, parents and teachers are seldom disinterested in this situation. Instead of teaching children a rational morality, they "follow the dictates of their own super-ego. . . . In the education of the child they are severe and exacting. They have forgotten the difficulties of their own childhood, and are glad to be able to identify themselves fully at last with their own parents, who in their day subjected them to such severe restraints."[10]

In this way, not merely the sins but also the prejudices and psychological abnormalities of the parents are passed on to the children from generation to generation.

The good teacher is one who is able to break into this vicious circle and establish a wholly personal relationship with his pupil, one which is based on love and understanding for the unique personality which has been entrusted to his care. Such a teacher will not attempt to impose on his pupil arbitrary conceptions of "good" and "bad," which the child is unable to feel or understand (and which therefore lead to a state

---

[9] *New Introductory Lectures,* p. 87.
[10] *Ibid.,* p. 90.

of tension or disunity which is one origin of neurosis). He will ignore the whole system of "make-believe" with its rewards and punishments, its constraints and inhibitions. He will try instead to establish a relationship of reciprocity and trust between himself and his pupil, and one of co-operation and mutual aid between all the individuals within his care. The teacher should identify himself with the pupil in the same degree that the pupil identifies himself with the teacher, and he should probably endeavour to make this process, on the pupil's part, more conscious than it would normally be. What is required is the give and take of a mutual relationship. The child is likely to develop his side of the relationship in the natural course of his development: from the teacher a more deliberate approach will be necessary, for he must really identify himself with the other person and feel and do as he does. The teacher sees the situation from both ends, the pupil from one only. In this way the teacher gradually learns to distinguish and anticipate the real needs of his pupil, and only in this way is it possible for him to accomplish those tasks which Freud assigns to the teacher—to recognize the child's disposition, to understand his mind, to love him and to preserve effective authority over him.[11]

---

[11] Godwin, in an essay "On the Obtaining of Confidence," long ago expressed this truth in words which have lost none of their relevance to this discussion:

If any man desire to possess himself of the most powerful

7. THE PERSON AND THE GROUP

If this right relationship is developed between the teacher and his pupil, and the teacher thus becomes the focus of a group of pupils who love him and trust him, it is then easy to establish the precepts of mutual aid within that group. This means that within the group—the class, the house, the school—a relationship of reciprocity has been formed which can take the place of those relationships of constraint that are normal in traditional methods of education.

If this feeling of trust in the teacher were the only psychological motive active within such a group, it is possible that complications due to envy and rivalry would ensue. But actually the group develops spontaneously a social life and cohesion which are inde-

engine that can be applied to the purpose of education, if he would find the ground upon which he must stand to enable himself to move the whole substance of the mind, he will probably find it in sympathy. Great power is not necessarily a subject of abuse. A wise preceptor would probably desire to be in possession of great power over the mind of his pupil, though he would use it with economy and diffidence. He would therefore seek by all honest arts to be admitted into his confidence, that so the points of contact between them may be more extensively multiplied, that he may not be regarded by the pupil as a stranger of the outer court of the temple, but that his image may mix itself with his pleasures, and be made the companion of his recreations. (*Enquirer*, pp. 124–5.)

pendent of the teacher. The spontaneous emergence
of groups among children has been studied by educationalists like Jean Piaget and Susan Isaacs, and a
social experiment on a large scale which covers the
whole development of the individual was conducted
at the Peckham Health Centre,[12] with results which
fully support this thesis.

The importance of this development, in the life of
the child, is that it leads the child *by natural stages*
from a self-centered state of egotism to an attitude
of social co-operation. There is then no question of
forcing the child to recognize and accept a moral

----

[12] Innes H. Pearse and Lucy H. Crocker, *The Peckham Experiment, a Study in the Living Structure of Society* (London, 1943),
pp. 291-2:

'Community' is not formed merely by the aggregation of persons assembled for the convenience of sustaining some ul-
terior purpose, as in a housing estate connected with a single
industry; not by the aggregation of individuals kept in con-
tiguity by the compulsion of necessity, as in 'special areas'
wrecked by unemployment; nor held together, as in some
social settlements, by the doubtful adhesive of persuasion;
nor indeed meeting the needs of war time as in 'Communal
Feeding,' 'Communal Nurseries.' Its characteristic is that it
is the result of a *natural functional organization in society,*
which brings *its own* intrinsic impetus to ordered growth and
development. In our understanding, 'community' is built up of
homes linked with *society* through a functional zone of mutuality. As it grows in mutuality of synthesis it *determines its
own* anatomy and physiology, according to biological law. A
community is thus a specific 'organ' of the body of society,
and is formed of living and growing cells—the homes of
which it is composed.

code whose justice it cannot appreciate. That abstract "sense of duty" is wholly outside the child's mental range: the child can only be coerced into its observance. But that sense of "playing the game" which emerges when children evolve their own activities is a real thing: it is a felt relationship between little human beings who must co-operate to achieve their common aim. And to achieve this aim they must create a pattern—the rules of the game which give coherence and form to their activities. In such spontaneously evolved patterns, giving pleasures and satisfaction to the growing animal instincts and desires, lies hidden the pattern of a society in which all persons are free, but freely consenting to a common purpose.

It is impossible to exaggerate the fundamental nature of this aspect of education, which I have called *initiation*. At this stage of life a choice must be made which inevitably dictates the form our society will take. In one direction we can institute objective codes of conduct and morality to which our children are introduced before the age of understanding and to which they are compelled to conform by a system of rewards and punishments. That way leads to an authoritarian society, governed by laws and sanctioned by military power. It is the kind of society in which most of the world now lives, ridden by neuroses, full of envy and avarice, ravaged by war and disease.

In the other direction we can avoid all coercive codes of morality, all formal conceptions of "right" and "wrong." For a morality of obedience we can substitute a morality of attachment or reciprocity, that living together in perfect charity which was once the ideal of Christianity. Believing that the spontaneous life developed by children among themselves gives rise to a discipline infinitely nearer to that inner accord or harmony which is the mark of the virtuous man, we can aim at making our teachers the friends rather than the masters of their pupils; as teachers they will not lay down readymade rules, but will encourage their children to carry out their own co-operative activities, and thus spontaneously to elaborate their own rules. Discipline will not be imposed, but discovered—discovered as the right, economical and harmonious way of action. We can avoid the competitive evils of the examination system, which merely serves to reinforce the egocentrism inherent in the child: we can eliminate all ideas of rewards and punishments, substituting a sense of the collective good of the community, to which reparation for shortcomings and selfishness will be obviously due and freely given. In all things, moral and intellectual, we should act on the belief that we really possess only what we have conquered ourselves—that we are made perfect by natural habits, but slaves by social conventions; and that until we have become accustomed to beauty we are not capable of truth and goodness, for by beauty we mean the principle of harmony which is the given order of the physical universe, to which we conform and live, or which we reject and die.

8. THE FREEDOM OF THE SCHOOL

The reader who has followed me with agreement so far must now be prepared for some logical consequences that are at variance with the general trend of progressive thought. Progress in education throughout the civilized world has been for the most part conceived in terms of "national systems," and all our endeavours have been to make such systems more and more inclusive and more and more standardized. If only the system is perfect, we have argued, the products will be as good as possible.

We might have proceeded in other ways: we might, for example, have concentrated on the training of teachers, and having made that perfect, said to them: "Go out into the world, and wherever there are children to listen to you, in village halls and at street corners, on highways and byways, gather little children round you and teach them as once Christ taught them." We might, that is to say, have thought of teachers as missionaries rather than as masters; and who would venture to say that the state of the world would then have been worse than it is?

There are still other possibilities. Instead of entrusting the education of children to bureaucratic organizations divorced from the main business of life, we might have developed the apprenticeship system, and made education a preparation for vocation—the doctors educating some children, the lawyers others, the engineers others, the weavers and the miners still others. Each guild or trade would have taken in its future apprentices from the beginning, much as, even now, some religious orders supervise the education from early years of those children destined to become novices. Instead of these and other possibilities, we have established *national* or *state* systems of education. In some countries, England and the United States among them, a few schools still manage to exist outside the official orbit, but unless, like some of the so-called "public" schools of England, they are richly endowed, they fight a losing battle against the increasing ubiquity and efficiency of the state schools.

There is no need to describe this system, because we all have experience of it. But few people are conscious of its dangers. These are of two distinct kinds.

The first of these dangers was anticipated by Godwin, and I cannot do better than repeat his warning:

The project of a national education ought uniformly to be discouraged on account of its obvious alliance with national government. This

is an alliance of a more formidable nature than
the old and much contested alliance of church
and state. Before we put so powerful a machine
under the direction of so ambiguous an agent, it
behooves us to consider well what it is that we do.
Government will not fail to employ it to strength-
en its hands and perpetuate its institutions. If we
could even suppose the agents of government not
to propose to themselves an object which will be
apt to appear in their eyes not merely innocent
but meritorious, the evil would none the less happen. Their views as institutors of a system of education will not fail to be analogous to their views
in their political capacity: the data upon which
their conduct as statesmen is vindicated will be
the data upon which their instructions are
founded. It is not true that our youth ought to
be instructed to venerate the Constitution, however excellent; they should be instructed to venerate truth, and the Constitution only so far as
it corresponded with their independent deductions of truth. Had the scheme of a national
education been adopted when despotism was
most triumphant, it is not to be believed that it
could have forever stifled the voice of truth. But
it would have been the most formidable and profound contrivance for that purpose that imagination can suggest. Still, in the countries where
liberty chiefly prevails, it is reasonably to be assumed that there are important errors, and a national education has the most direct tendency to

perpetuate those errors and to form all minds upon one model.[13]

It is difficult to realize that this passage was published in 1793, before the growth of national states like France and Germany, and before the institution of totalitarian regimes which make this very use which Godwin feared of their educational system. In Great Britain certain safeguards were originally imposed, such as school managers and local educational authorities, but these bodies are gradually losing their independence, and recent legislation has virtually abolished their powers. A system of national education has become potentially a system of national propaganda, designed to inculcate certain attitudes and beliefs which *may* not correspond with our independent deductions of truth. National socialism in Germany, with its wild distortions of scientific truth and of historical fact, would not have survived so long had not the government utilized the national system of education for the dissemination of the party's doctrines. The same is true of the national communism established in Russia. To regularize and nationalize the instruments of education is merely to convert these instruments into weapons of dictatorship.

A second objection to a national system of education is psychological rather than political. Mankind is naturally differentiated into many types, and to

---

[13] *Political Justice,* VI, 8.

press all these types into the same mould must inevitably lead to distortions and repressions. Schools
should be of many kinds, following different methods
and catering to different dispositions. It might be
argued that even a totalitarian state must recognize
this principle, but the truth is that differentiation is
an organic process, the spontaneous and roving association of individuals for particular purposes. To divide and segregate is not the same as to join and
aggregate—it is just the opposite process. The whole
structure of education, as the natural process we
have envisaged, falls to pieces if we attempt to make
that structure rational or artificial.[14] Like life itself,
animal as well as human education must follow a

[14] Such "rational" organization is attempted in England by the
new Education Act. The division of secondary schools into three
types—grammar, technical and modern—represents artificial categories based on "aptitudes" determined by a cursory examination
held at the immature age of ten or eleven. Subsequent interchange
between these categories is legally possible, but administratively
difficult and therefore unlikely. The articulation proposed here is
regional or local, the smallest units being nursery schools, several
of which feed a primary school, of which in turn several feed a
secondary school—the schools increasing in size as they cater to
higher age groups and wider areas but always remaining "multi-
lateral" in their curricula. Only in this way can we hope to retain
that dialectical interplay between diverse dispositions which is the
basis of a natural character-formation. The vocational segregation
of "like-minded" children from the age of eleven onward can lead
only to intellectual dullness and social apathy. Birds of a feather
flock together, but it is now proposed that they should be caged
together.

principle of organic consistency: we must *feel our way* to the right units. Free and healthy institutions will emerge from the biological actualities and practical activities of man. Among these we shall find institutions in which children can mature, the principle of growth innate in each one of them, while at the same time they are initiated into the fellowship of their familiars.

9. A COMMUNITY OF INDIVIDUALS

Freud was never tired of warning us of the thinness and brittleness of the shell we call civilization. In one place he writes:

> Civilized society, which exacts good conduct and does not trouble about the impulses underlying it, has thus won over to obedience a great many people who are not thereby following the dictates of their own nature. Encouraged by this success, society has suffered itself to be led into straining the normal standard to the highest possible point, and thus it has forced its members into yet greater estrangement from their instinctual dispositions. They are consequently subjected to an unceasing suppression of instincts, the resulting strain of which betrays itself in the most remarkable phenomena of reaction and compensation formations. . . . Anyone thus com-

pelled to act continually in the sense of precepts which are not the expression of instinctual inclinations is living, psychologically speaking, beyond his means, and might objectively be designated a hypocrite, whether this difference is clearly known to him or not. It is undeniable that our contemporary civilization is extraordinarily favourable to the production of this form of hypocrisy. One might venture to say that it is based on such hypocrisy, and that it should have to submit to far-reaching modifications if people were to undertake to live in accordance with the psychological truth.[15]

---

[15] *Collected Papers,* IV, "Thoughts for the Times on War and Death." Schiller said very much the same in his *Letters upon the Aesthetical Education of Man:*

In this way individual concrete life is gradually extinguished, in order that the abstract whole may prolong its miserable existence, and the state remains forever a stranger to its citizens, because it is nowhere present to their feelings. Compelled to reduce to some order the multiplicity of its citizens by classifying them, and only to know humanity through representation at second hand, the governing classes end by altogether losing sight of their citizens, reducing them to some figment of the mind. Meanwhile the subject classes cannot but welcome coldly laws which are so little addressed to them personally. In the end, tired of a bondage which the state does so little to lighten, positive society disintegrates—a fate which has long ago overcome most European states. It dissolves into a moral state of nature, in which the public authority is nothing more than a class, hated and betrayed by those who make its existence necessary, respected only by those who can do without it.

Freud himself never ventured to outline those "far-reaching modifications" which society would have to undergo for the sake of psychological truth, which I think we may assume is the same thing as psychological happiness. But he did indicate in unmistakable terms that he did not consider such necessary modifications to have been achieved under the collectivist systems of Russia and Germany.[16] For this reason Marxists have often condemned this great scientist as a reactionary, and it is true that by their insistence on the integrity of the family, for example, psychoanalysts find themselves in the company of conservative forces such as the Catholic Church. But they will not for this reason be deterred from stating the psychological truth, as they see it. The same scientific obligation will also lead them to side with those political forces which oppose the state as such. Already certain followers of Freud set drastic limits to the beneficial effects of state interference. For example, Dr. Edward Glover, the director of the Psychoanalytical Institute of Great Britain, does not hesitate to declare that "state worship is a form of fetishism derived from the displacement of family dependence," and suggests further that "however useful the state may be in the regulation of material things it is nevertheless a backward and superstitious

---

[16] Cf. especially *New Introductory Lectures,* Lecture XXXV, "A Philosophy of Life."

organization." Its true function is "to promote and strengthen in every possible way the status of the family within which civilization is born and maintained and by which it is transmitted."[17]

It is important to realize that these psychologists are not recommending a particular policy on ideological grounds; they are dealing with the psychological and the physiological health of the human organism, and they assert that this health cannot be maintained unless certain conflicts which are the product of modern civilization are avoided. These conflicts arise when in the course of his childhood and youth man finds that he has to adjust himself to unreal systems of law, morality and convention—systems which are unreal because they are remote and abstract, not necessarily in conformity with his biological needs or with the general pattern of nature. Man is born free; and everywhere he is in *mental* chains. Neurosis, crime, insanity—these are but so many symptoms of a disorder that is basic to our form of society. Man is ill-adjusted from the nursery up, and this ill-adjustment and consequent unhappiness is not something which can be prevented or removed by individual analysis—it is a group disorder and can be removed only by "far-reaching modifications" of our contemporary civilization.

To demand freedom in education, autonomy in

---

[17] "State Parentalism," *New English Weekly*, March 23, 1944.

the school and self-government in industry is not to be inspired by any vague ideal of liberation. What we seek is a discipline and a morality as formal and as fixed as any preached by church or state. But our law is given in nature, is discoverable by scientific method, and, as Aristotle points out, human beings are adapted by nature to receive this law. Because we are so adapted, freedom, which is a vague concept to so many people, becomes a perfectly real and vivid principle, because it is a habit to which we are pre-conditioned by biological elements in our physical frame and nervous constitution.

Education, from this point of view, is an undeveloped science. To discover, for example, the degree of poise and co-ordination in the muscular system of the body is an art which has never yet been defined and practised. Harmony within the family, harmony within the social group, harmony within and among nations —these are no less psycho-physiological problems, questions of pattern and practice, of adjustment to natural proportions and conformity to natural harmonies.

Each individual begins life as a dynamic unity. Into that original unity tensions and distortions are introduced by an unconscious and largely alien environment. It is alien because it is unconscious. Unless we were motivated by hatred towards the human race, we could not consciously introduce those abstract systems of law and morality on which the evolving body and soul of the person, born to potential unity and beauty, are disastrously stretched and deformed.

I do not pretend to know what are the exact precepts of a morality of love and mutual aid: I doubt if they can be formulated more explicitly than they were long ago in the Sermon on the Mount. But life, which is an organic growth, cannot be lived according to an abstract formula of words, but only to a pattern, and not to a pattern in the abstract sense of a defined form, but only to a living, evolving form, which obeys rules, not in stasis, but in growth. Life is movement: we cannot halt it for a moment without killing it. The pattern is visible only in time. We can give pattern to our span of years, but we cannot, without death or distortion, give life to a pattern of law, to any "purely verbal, symbolic system of behaviour."[18] The basis of a living community, the basis of individual happiness, is physiological: it is only in so far as this physiological basis has unity with nature (*physis* = nature) that society itself can have harmony and health. It is in small units—in the family circle, in the classroom and in the school—that this harmony and health must be first achieved. In so far as some abstraction called the state interferes with the integrity of these groups—and by their integrity we mean their capacity for spontaneous growth—in that degree the

---

[18] Dr. Trigant Burrow.

state is denying life and health to its citizens. Freedom is simply space for spontaneous action: men live in communities solely to secure that space.

10. SUMMARY

I hope I may now expect from my reader a clearer understanding of what is meant by "freedom in education." We can now see that it is more exact to speak of "education for freedom" or "education for peace." But this is a misleading slogan unless we remember the means, which is the discipline of art, the only discipline to which the senses naturally submit. Art, as we have seen, is a discipline which the senses seek in their intuitive perception of form, of harmony, of proportion, of the integrity or wholeness of any experience. It is also the discipline of the tool and the material—the discipline imposed by pencil or pen, by the loom or the potter's wheel, by the physical nature of paint, textiles, wood, stone or clay.

But the point about such discipline is that it is innate: it is part of our physiological constitution, and is there to be encouraged and matured. It does not have to be imposed by the schoolmaster or the drill sergeant: it is not a kind of physical torture. It is a faculty within the child which responds to sympathy and love, to the intelligent anticipation of impulses and trends in the individuality of the child. For this reason the teacher must be primarily a person and not a pedagogue, a friend rather than a master or mistress, an infinitely patient collaborator. Put in a drier and more pedantic way, the aim of education is to discover the child's psychological type, and to allow each type its natural line of development, its natural form of integration. That is the real meaning of freedom in education.

The art of children is supremely important for this very reason: it is the earliest and most exact index to the child's individual psychology. Once the psychological tendency or trend of a child is known, its own individuality can be developed by the discipline of art, till it has its own form and beauty, which is its unique contribution to the beauties of human nature. This, of course, is the antithesis of those totalitarian doctrines of education (not confined to totalitarian countries) which strive to impose a unique concept of human nature on the infinite variety of human persons.

A child's art, therefore, is its passport to freedom, to the full fruition of all its gifts and talents, to its true and stable happiness in adult life. Art leads the child out of itself. It may begin as a lonely individual activity, as the self-absorbed scribbling of a baby on a piece of paper. But the child scribbles in order to communicate its inner world to a sympathetic spectator, to the parent from whom it expects a sympathetic response.

Too often, alas, it receives only indifference or ridicule. Nothing is more crushing to the infant spirit than a parent's or a teacher's contempt for those creative efforts of expression. That is one aspect of a process which disgraces the whole of our intellectualized civilization and which, in my opinion, is the root cause of our social disintegration. We sow the seeds of disunity in the nursery and the classroom, with our superior adult conceit. We divide the intelligence from the sensibility of our children, create split-men (schizophrenics, to give them a psychological name), and then discover that we have no social unity.

We begin our life in unity—the physical unity of the mother and child, to which corresponds the emotional unity of love. We should build on that original unity, extending it first to the family, where the seeds of hatred are so easily and so often sown, and then to the school, and so by stages to the farm, the workshop, the village and the whole community. But the basis of unity at each successive stage, as at the first stage, is creativity. We unite to create, and the pattern of creation is in nature, and we discover and conform to this pattern by all the methods of artistic activity—by music, by dancing and drama, but also by working together and living together, for, in a sane civilization, these too are arts of the same natural pattern.

II

EDUCATION IN THINGS

1. A WORLD OF THINGS

I HAVE ALREADY QUOTED one of those aphorisms which keep a book like *Emile* forever vital: "Keep the child dependent on things only." I should now like to develop the implications of that formula, giving to it a meaning which Rousseau himself, perhaps, would not have wholly approved.

While engaged in making some notes for this chapter, I picked up a book that had just been published in England, and which had no apparent connection with our subject—it was the *Letters of Eric Gill*. Eric Gill was a friend of mine, and I owe much to the fierce challenges which he often threw at me in friendly conversation or public debate. I do not remember that we ever discussed the problem of education, but on opening the volume of his letters I found one addressed to his son-in-law which, without any reference to Rousseau, and, I suspect,

without any knowledge of Rousseau's phrase, re-
states the problem in contemporary terms. It is
rather a long text, perhaps, but it is too much to
the point to reject or shorten. In schools as we
know them, Gill wrote:

> there is on one hand:
>> *Book education*—therefore thoughts, words,
>> ideas, reading *about* it, writing *about* it,
>> learning *about* it, and *exams* about it *(men-
>> tal* discipline, *intellectual* discipline)
> and on the other:
>> *Games education*—therefore actions, physical
>> development, combative enthusiasm, loyalty
>> development—the 'team spirit'. Personal
>> prowess, pride in oneself—self-respect . . .
>> (in fact, *moral* discipline, discipline of the
>> *will*).
> But on neither hand is there any education in
> *things!*
>> There is no *poetic experience.*
>> Intellect is trained almost entirely by books.
>> Will is trained almost entirely by games . . .
> But . . . we live in a world of *things.* Making
> things is a large part of man's life—*any* man's,
> and certainly the majority of men are *operatives*
> of one kind or another. And yet there is no edu-
> cation in things—no education in poetic experi-
> ence. We grab an idea, a concept, an abstrac-
> tion, a representation, i.e., we train our *intellects.*
> We grab balls and bats and one another's an-

kles, i.e., we train our wills. But we grab no *thing*. No thing *as such* and for itself, no *being*— only thoughts *about* things, only actions in *relation* to things. Poet, *poiesis*, *maker*—grasper of *things*, reality as knowable by *experience* of it. Art, artistry (from cats' meat to cathedrals) is all a matter of poetry, grasping reality, grasping things.

It is rather a repetitive text, perhaps, but the state of complacency, of complete blindness to facts which stare us in the face, is such that only the repeated blows of a chiseller's mallet, such as Gill used in his daily work, can get them into our heads. There are a few simple but tremendously important truths about education which are ignored, not because we can dispose of them, deny them, but rather because the recognition of them would upset the whole scale of our *social* values—destroy, as we might say, our accepted pattern of behaviour. Why we should cling so desperately, so irrationally, to social values or patterns of behaviour which again and again have led us to war and unemployment and other miseries is more than our present science of psychology can explain. That science can only suggest a therapy, a cure for ills it cannot adequately diagnose—but it has gone so far as to admit that in the immediate circumstances of our lives the pursuit of any activities that engage the sensuous faculties in practical skills, and that

lead to a deeper appreciation of beauty or grace, are
obviously desirable as an antidote to the nervous and
physical diseases of our almost wholly mechanized
civilization. But surely we can agree that for this
body of society of which we are all members, no less
than for the body of the individual human being,
prevention is better than cure. Nothing, from this
point of view, is more degrading to the dignity and
spiritual value of art than to regard it as merely a
form of therapy, a medicine to be administered in
doses only when the patient is sick. Art is rather
an expression of health: it is exuberance, exhilaration,
ecstasy. But again, it is not the expression of an
exceptional state of health such as words like these
might suggest: art is, or should be, the normal sensuous quality or virtue of all that we make or manufacture. Since when, we must ask, did art become a
thing apart, an activity which we now associate only
with leisure, or with recreation?

I shall have more to say later about the problem
of leisure in our civilization, but for the moment let
us note that its common use is directly related to that
gap in education described by Gill.

Leisure is a word that has subtly and slowly changed
its meaning during the course of the last hundred
years. It used to mean no more than "time" or "opportunity." "If your leisure serv'd," says one of
Shakespeare's characters, "I would speak with you."

Phrases which we still use, such as "at your leisure," preserve this original meaning.

But when, as nowadays, we speak of the *problem* of leisure, we are not thinking of securing time or opportunity to do something: we have time on our hands, and the problem is how to fill it. Leisure no longer signifies a space with some difficulty secured against the pressure of events: rather it signifies a pervasive emptiness for which we must invent occupations. Leisure is a vacuum, a desperate state of vacancy—a vacancy of mind and body. It has been handed over to the sociologists and the psychologists: to such specialists it is more than a problem—it is a disease.

I can think of no change so symptomatic of our degeneracy, our civilized dis-ease, as this change in the meaning of "leisure." The habit of thought it represents is so deeply ingrained that I fear it is going to be difficult for me to make clear the possibility of a different attitude, of a different way of life.

2. WORK AND PLAY

The existence of most people is divided into two phases, as distinct as day and night. We call them *work* and *play*. We work for so many hours a day, and when we have allowed the necessary minimum

for such activities as eating and shopping, the rest
we spend in various activities which we call *recreations,* an elegant word which indicates that we do
not even play in our hours of leisure, but spend them
in various forms of passive enjoyment which we call
entertainment—not playing baseball, but watching
baseball games; not drama, but theatre-going; not
walking, but riding in an automobile.

We have, therefore, not only a hard-and-fast distinction between work and play, but an equally hard-and-fast distinction between active play and passive
entertainment. It is, I suppose, the decline of active
play—of amateur sport—and the enormous growth of
purely receptive entertainment which have given rise
to a sociological interest in the problem. If the greater
part of the population, instead of indulging in healthy
sports, spend their hours of leisure watching an animated screen in their homes or in dark and crowded
cinemas, there will inevitably be a decline in health
and physique. And in addition there will be a psychological problem, for we have yet to trace the mental
and moral consequences of a prolonged diet of sentimental or sensational "features." There is, if we are
optimistic, the possibility that the diet is too thin and
unnourishing to have much permanent effect on anybody. Nine films or television features out of ten seem
to leave absolutely no impress on the mind or imagination of those who see them: few people can give a
coherent account of the film they saw the week before

last, and at longer intervals they must rely on the management to see that they do not sit through the same film twice.

On the same level of passive entertainment are most of the programs provided by sound broadcasting and most of the reading provided by the book clubs and circulating libraries. I know that there are good things broadcast almost every day, and not every novel is a sentimental best-seller. But I am not really concerned with the quality of passive entertainment; from my present point of view I see no great difference between the person who sits through a film and the person who sits in an armchair at home and listens to a symphony. The passive absorption of repeated doses of music, or of poetry or any other sensuous drug, does not seem to me to be necessarily a good thing. The arts were originally a communal celebration: they were created for people gathered together to dance, or sing, or worship. They gained as much from this communion as they gave: the form and the effect were enhanced by physical contagion, by common enjoyment.

I might as well confess at this point that I daily grow more suspicious of what I can only call exhibitionist culture. Exhibitions of painting and sculpture, of French tapestries or Australasian totems; concerts of classical music, of modern music, of Chinese music; operas from Vienna or ballet from Russia—yes, they are all very entertaining, a little exhausting if we care to keep up with the accelerating pace of it all; and no doubt it does increase the curious collection of odd impressions, of disconnected facts and half-remembered names, which we keep in some corner of our cerebellum and call knowledge—and which we dig up from this cloudy and over-crowded receptacle when we want to display our "culture." But what does it all mean in the terms of the vital reality which is our daily behaviour and immediate happiness? Very little that I can see.

We have to live art if we would be affected by art. We have to paint rather than look at paintings, to play instruments rather than go to concerts, to dance and sing and act ourselves, engaging all our senses in the ritual and discipline of the arts. Then something may begin to happen to us: to work upon our bodies and our souls.

That is my first point: entertainment must be active, participated in, practised. It is then more properly called *play,* and as such it is a natural use of leisure. In that sense it stands in contrast to *work,* and is usually regarded as an activity which alternates with work. It is there that the final and most fundamental error enters into our conception of daily life.

Work itself is not a single concept. We say quite generally that we work in order to make a living: to earn, that is to say, sufficient tokens which we can exchange for food and shelter and all the other needs of our existence. But some of us work physically, tilling the land, minding the machines, digging the coal; others work mentally, keeping accounts, inventing machines, teaching and preaching, managing and governing. There does not seem to be any factor common to all these diverse occupations, except that they consume our time and leave us little leisure. But at different periods they have been differently regarded. Some work, such as mining, was once despised, and forced on slaves and prisoners of war. A miner is now a highly esteemed and relatively highly paid craftsman. Surgeons used to be on the level with barbers: theirs is now one of the most richly rewarded professions in the world. The social status of the actor has been completely transformed during the past two centuries. But though the constituent elements may shift from one level to another, the hierarchy remains fairly constant. The professions occupy one level, the merchant adventurers another (we now call them by a less romantic title), and below these are the skilled craftsmen and still lower, at the bottom of the pyramid, the unskilled labourers.

We may next observe that one man's profession or work is often another man's recreation or play. The merchant at the week-end becomes a hunter (he has not yet taken to mining); the clerk becomes a gardener; the machine-tender becomes a breeder of bull terriers. There is, of course, a sound instinct behind such transformations. The body and mind are unconsciously seeking compensation—muscular co-ordination, mental integration. But in many cases a dissociation is set up and the individual leads a double life—one half Jekyll, and the other half Hyde. There is a profound moral behind Stevenson's story, for the compensation which a disintegrated personality may seek will often be of an anti-social nature. The Nazi party, for example, in its early days was largely recruited from the bored—not so much from the unemployed as from the street-corner society of listless teen-agers.

Scientific studies have been made of street-corner society—the society out of which crime, gangsterism and fascism inevitably develop. It is a society with leisure—that is to say, spare time—and without compensatory occupation. It does not need a Satan to find mischief for such idle hands to do—idle hands will spontaneously itch to do something: muscles have a life of their own unless they are trained to purposeful actions. Actions, or rather *activities,* are the obvious reflex to leisure: they consume it, and leave the problem solved.

But work is also activity, and if we reach the conclusion that all our time must be filled with one activity or another, the distinction between work and play becomes rather meaningless, and what we mean by play is merely a change of occupation. We pass from one form of activity to another: one we call work, and for that we receive pay; the other we call play, and for that we receive no pay—on the contrary, we probably pay a subscription.

Let us now assume that the activity for which we are paid is an enjoyable one. Here we must be careful not to make false assumptions. There are many people who are "proud of their job," or in some sense satisfied with their position in the world, not because they find any enjoyment or satisfaction in the activity itself, but because it is well-paid, or ensures a position of prestige in society. I have met many people who are proud of their status, but they hate the sight of their office or place of work. Money and all it can buy, social privileges and a sense of superiority, give them a feeling of satisfaction or complacency which overwhelms the essential emptiness or boredom of their occupation.

3. THE CRAFTSMAN

These last are not the people I have in mind. Let us rather consider a craftsman who takes an endless delight in his work—he may be a surgeon, he may be a poet; he may be a ploughman or a plasterer. The question we must then ask is: Where does his work end, or his play begin? Will that craftsman put down his tools, to go and stand blankly at a street corner? Will he stop his operation halfway, to smoke a cigarette, to play a game of snooker? There is a fable re-

lated by Thoreau towards the end of *Walden* for a
different purpose which will serve to illustrate my
meaning here:

> There was an artist in the city of Kouroo who
> was disposed to strive after perfection. One day
> it came into his mind to make a staff. Having con-
> sidered that in an imperfect work time is an in-
> gredient, but into a perfect work time does not
> enter, he said to himself, it shall be perfect in all
> respects, though I should do nothing else in
> my life. He proceeded instantly to the forest for
> wood, being resolved that it should not be made
> of unsuitable material; and as he searched for and
> rejected stick after stick, his friends gradually
> deserted him, for they grew old in their works
> and died, but he grew not older by a moment.
> High singleness of purpose and resolution, and
> his elevated piety, endowed him, without his
> knowledge, with perennial youth. As he made no
> compromise with Time, Time kept out of his
> way, and only sighed at a distance because he
> could not overcome him. Before he had found a
> stick in all respects suitable the city of Kouroo
> was a hoary ruin, and he sat on one of its mounds
> to peel the stick. Before he had given it the
> proper shape the dynasty of the Candahars was
> at an end, and with the point of the stick he wrote
> the name of the last of that race in the sand,
> and then resumed his work. By the time he had
> smoothed and polished the staff Kalpa was no

longer the pole-star; and ere he had put on the ferrule and the head adorned with precious stones, Brahma had awoke and slumbered many times. But why do I stay to mention these things? When the finishing stroke was put to his work, it suddenly expanded before the eyes of the astonished artist into the fairest of all the creations of Brahma. He had made a new system in making a staff, a world with full and fair proportions; in which, though the old cities and dynasties had passed away, fairer and more glorious ones had taken their places. And now he saw by the heap of shavings still fresh at his feet, that, for him and his work, the former lapse of time had been an illusion, and that no more time had elapsed than is required for a single scintillation from the brain of Brahma to fall on and inflame the tinder of a mortal brain. The material was pure, and his art was pure; how could the result be other than wonderful?

Compare the singleness of purpose which this fable illustrates with the divided purposes of our average life, and you will see the drift of my argument. Thoreau went into the woods to demonstrate that "to maintain one's self on this earth is not a hardship but a pastime, if we will live simply and wisely"; he succeeded in his task, but his experiment would have died with him, and been lost to the world, but for the paper mills and printing presses which imply a very different kind of life for the majority of people. The difficulty is not to maintain one's self, but a society in which the self can expand and find its fulfilment.

Thoreau tried to obtain his freedom by abolishing work; the real solution is to combine freedom and work, and this can be done only by transforming work into play, or play into work. The craftsman can do this because he can *lose* himself in his work, by which we mean that he can engage all his faculties in the execution of his work—mind, muscle, vision, touch and judgment. The true craftsman has no leisure, but only rest and freedom; he is a player who has put down his instrument, to enjoy the sense of freedom, to relax, to indulge the senses, to meditate, to worship, to pray, and finally to die in peace of mind.

The craftsman is an anomaly in our modern mechanized society: he is almost extinct. The problem, therefore, is to introduce the emotional satisfactions of a craftsman's work into the industrial system which is our heritage. It is a problem with almost endless extensions, so complex that many thinkers who have tried to solve it have despaired, and cried out in their despair for a reversal of history, for the abolition of the system of machine production and a return to the system of handicrafts. Ruskin, Tolstoy, Morris, Gandhi, Gill—all these great men, with

impressive unanimity, have condemned our modern
society, and found no solution other than a return
to a peasant economy. They, too, would live simply
and wisely, like Thoreau in his wood by Walden Pond.

There are two factors which now make such a solution unrealistic. The machine has not left the world
as it found it. It has created a vast army to serve it—
the proletariat. In the British Isles alone the population doubled between 1830 and 1930—twenty mil-
lion extra human beings came into existence, to serve
the machines and to be fed and clothed by the
machines. Accompanying this expansion of population, there was a progressive increase in the standard of living—I do not mean so much in the amount
and quality of food, as in comforts and conveniences
which we would never willingly surrender—swift communications, electric power, clean cities and discreet
sanitation. It may be, as Eric Gill believed (and as
Jean Giono, the great French writer who has also
written profoundly on these problems, also believes),
that these benefits have been purchased too dearly:
that moral and physical health will never be restored
to the world until the last tractor has rusted into the
soil and the peasant once more goes to bed by candle-
light, having spent the day carting his home-made
compost to the hand-ploughed fields. But what about
the millions of extra "hands" which now tend the
machines? Emigration? But emigration is no solution

unless you have a machine-civilization, which alone makes it possible for mankind to develop the waste spaces of the world.

Apart from such considerations (and I admit the argument is not complete), there is something radically wrong in such defeatism. A civilization can, of course, take a wrong turning, and its peoples find too late that catastrophe has overtaken them. It may be that we are on a steep incline which leads to such a disaster. But we cannot save ourselves by turning back. There is no single instance of a civilization in the past that turned back on its tracks and saved itself. But there are plenty of instances of such "a failure of nerve"—of civilizations that have not dared to go forward, or even to stand firm. I do not suppose that there are any simple explanations of the decline of civilizations, but such causes as there are combine to exhibit a lack of faith in the future, of zest in the present.

We should attempt, therefore, to control the machine before we destroy it, or let it destroy us. Up to the present we have exercised very little social control on the machine. We have had our Factory Acts and workshop regulations; we now have some timid attempts at town planning and the planned location of industries. But we have never ventured to say the machine shall go thus far and no farther; the machine shall do this, but not that; the machine shall be put here, but not there. The whole development of machine production has been sporadic and uncontrolled. It has proliferated: it has not been rationed.

4. DECENTRALIZATION

I believe that the greatest evils that flow from machine production are evils of location and distribution. The centralization of industry was a consequence of the localization of power—on the river bank, near the colliery, near the railway. Electrification and the internal-combustion engine have almost completely destroyed the *raison d'être* of such centralization. The factory can now be located in the village, and, moreover, it can itself be split up and decentralized, component parts being made in half a dozen different localities and assembled in another. Henry Ford, who was no fool in such matters, came to the conclusion, towards the end of his life, that his great centralized factory at Detroit was a dinosaur —an obsolete monster. He began to advocate a widely spread network of village workshops. In such workshops workers would be healthier: they would have their gardens and even their farms, and live the balanced life of the medieval craftsman. Vitality would return to the villages: the antagonism of town and country, peasantry and proletariat, would disap-

pear: a social unity, such as we have not known for
centuries, would be re-established.

Such villages already exist—in countries like Swit-
zerland and Sweden. I know one or two in England,
where the cottages are grouped round a church, a
pub, and a chair factory. But there are obvious limits
to such decentralization: the factories of Birmingham
would need more villages than can be found in the
county of Warwick, and instead of a relatively concentrated Black Country, we do not want one vast
Grey Country.

The problem is more difficult in some parts of the
United States, where the village, in any organic sense,
has never existed. But the village is an expression of
a given economic system, and if you change the
system into one that requires the village, villages will
soon spring up, even in Michigan. Frank Lloyd
Wright's "broad-acre city" is the alternative ideal—
a city so decentralized that it is virtually a chain of
villages.

I am convinced that decentralization is the physical
prerequisite of any solution of what we call the problem of leisure. It is not the human soul in its freedom that craves entertainment and the dissipation of
boredom: it is that soul crowded into cities, cut off
from the soil and the seasons, deprived of natural
alternations of satisfying activities. The city is literal-
ly a complex, and from that complex arises a vast

social neurosis of which this "problem of leisure" is but one of the symptoms.

It will need more than a physical reorientation of industry to cure that neurosis. There must also take place a psychical reorientation, a reintegration of the personality, a healing of the social consciousness. Something may be achieved in this direction by a distribution of ownership, or responsibility. We need the decentralization not only of industry itself, but also of the powers and responsibilities of industry. That kind of decentralization is as essential as physical decentralization, but obviously it would be dangerous if it merely led to the creation of a number of closed corporations, all brotherly love within, but all hatred and suspicion towards similar corporations in other industries. The sectarian persecutions and conflicts which developed within the Christian church warn us that a common faith may be a source of division unless we have first the physical and psychological bases of mutual aid. Our greatest task is the building of such bases, and we can carry it through, in my opinion, only by a process of education, but a process of education that will bear little relation to what we now call education.

Present systems of education might be generally described as *partitive*. Their tendency is not to unite but to divide. They divide in the first place because they establish a hierarchy or caste system, not only splitting children into age groups—infant, primary, secondary, technical, commercial and university—but decreeing that certain tests should determine the right of an individual child to proceed beyond a particular stage. Within each group similar tests and examinations determine the place of the individual child within the group. All these tests and examinations have the effect of pitting child against child in a grim struggle for places, and the division of any local community of children into groups determined by these tests further accentuates the sense of social division, of disunity.

Naturally, the process of education has to be organized, and a certain amount of "herding" is the inevitable accompaniment of overcrowded schools and overworked teachers. But what I am stressing is that, altogether apart from such questions of organization, there exists a deliberate policy of grading by intelligence tests. The more democratic we try to make the process of education, the more drastic these partitive procedures become. In England, for example, there is a test at the age of eleven plus which determines whether a child shall proceed to a secondary education or not, and this is creating a social division just as decisive as any that formerly existed between rich and poor, bourgeois and proletariat, upper class and lower class. Formerly social differences were determined by inherited wealth, or blood; they are now determined by inherited intelligence and regulated by a national educational system. That, at least, is the ideal of the national educational systems, and it may be that if some form of social hierarchy is desirable, or inevitable, one based on intelligence tests is superior to one based on inherited wealth. But even when functioning perfectly, such a system would still be partitive, establishing divisions rather than creating unity. There is, perhaps, no likelihood of a social hierarchy based on intelligence ever coming into being. Class distinctions have never been rational distinctions—they have always been based on irrational instincts and prejudices. A social order based on intelligence tests would cut right across many deeply rooted customs and vested interests. This would be true even of a society like the United States of America, where a democratic ideology prevails, and where there is certainly no intention to educate for class differences. I base this bold assertion on a book by three American authors. The title of the book is *Who Shall Be Educated? The Challenge of Unequal Opportunities*,[1] and the authors—two of them members of the Committee on Human Development, University of Chicago—after making a sociological survey of the schools in the United States, come to the conclusion that these schools,

functioning in a society with basic inequalities, facilitate the rise of a few from lower to higher

---

[1] W. Lloyd Warner, Robert J. Havinghurst, and Martin B. Loeb (London, 1956).

levels, but continue to serve the social system by keeping down many people who try for higher places. The teacher, the school administrator, the school board, as well as the students themselves, play their role to hold people in their places in our social structure. . . . The American school . . . reflects the socio-economic order in everything it does; in what it teaches, whom it teaches, who does the teaching, who does the hiring and the firing of the teachers, and what the children learn in and out of the classroom. . . . It is apparent that the high-school curriculum is a mechanism which helps perpetuate our class order.

Convincing evidence is brought forward to show that even in these democratic States of America, the educational system serves to preserve divisions rather than to promote unity.

Such social consequences of prevailing methods of education are not my main concern at the moment, but in so far as the unity of group consciousness is disrupted by education, to that extent it remains difficult to prevent the growth of social neurosis. But even supposing that the caste system which results from educational differentiation could be avoided, there still remains the fundamental educational problem: What kind of education will promote social union?

The answer is, of course, the same kind of education as that which promotes personal integrity. Education should always embrace the one and the many, the person and the group; and any phase of education which tends to emphasize the person against the group, or the group against the person, is obviously disruptive. Among these disruptive agencies I would place, not only the examination system and the systematic categories which are based on it, but, in a still more general sense, the whole ideal of modern education.

That ideal, as I have already said, is intellectual. It tends to become even narrower than that: the ideal in Great Britain and generally in Western Europe, Russia and the United States, is scientific. Even in subjects which used to be described as "liberal"— philosophy, literature and history—the spirit of teaching becomes increasingly "objective" or "positive," and all questions of "value" are rigidly excluded.

5. SOCIAL VIRTUE

What is thus excluded, in education generally, is the whole province of moral values. I agree with Gill that to a limited extent a discipline of the will is given in games education. I do not deplore the time given to games in our schools—on the contrary, it is often the only time well spent. But the moral discipline thus inculcated is of very limited duration—it

has no depth, it does not involve the imagination or
the emotional life in any profound sense. Games morality, the team spirit, has become indeed just one
more social convention—though to be "a good
sport" generally means to behave like a human being
rather than as a conventional citizen—in other words,
to disregard "morality." But "morality," in the sense
of a code of right and wrong, has to be distinguished
from the moral values of good and evil. Morality itself has been intellectualized, codified, and made a
matter of rational judgment instead of spontaneous
action. Moral education in the ancient world, when
Plato and Aristotle handled the theme, meant the
learning of something like good manners or good
form, good doing and good making; it was a dynamic
concept, a concept of nobility, of wisdom, of courage.
The object of moral education was expressed in the
one word *virtue*. Education, according to Plato,
should never be conceived with any narrow vocational
purpose. Education is rather "that schooling from
boyhood in goodness which inspires the recipient with
passionate and ardent desire to become a perfect
citizen."[2] Any other kind of education he regarded
as vulgar and illiberal.

Social union, social discipline, social morale—whatever we like to call that sense of belonging to one
another, of living in perfect brotherhood—that is or

---

[2] *Laws*, 643.

should be the aim of education. I do not pretend to
know what precise steps we should take, here and
now, to secure that kind of aim in education; but I
am quite sure that our existing systems of education
lead right away from social union, dissolve the subtle
bonds of love and fellowship, and leave us a nerve-
ridden aggressive herd.

Here and there we find experiments which point the
way. In England there is now a fairly widely diffused
awareness of the problem among educationists. As
yet practical reforms have become effective only in
a few sporadic instances, but there are very active
societies for Education Through Art, mentioned in
the prefatory section of this book. Their enthusiasm
is spreading the gospel throughout the world. Against
them is not only the existing system of education with
all its ramifications, all its vested interests and traditional practices, but also the social system itself
with its professional codes, its standards of rectitude
and knowledge.

Outside the educational sphere there are other
significant movements. The Peckham Health Centre,
which I have already mentioned, was an experiment
that came to an untimely end for lack of financial
support, but not before it had demonstrated in a
remarkable way the *physical* regeneration that follows
on the achievement of a group consciousness.[3] There

---

[3] Cf. *Biologists in Search of Material. An Interim Report on
the Pioneer Health Centre, Peckham* (London, 1938).

are many more experiments of an educational or psychological character being carried out in various parts of the world, only they lack co-ordination, they lack a common philosophy and aim. But there is among them a fairly conscious realization that the key to individual happiness and social unity is a certain kind of education. It is not sufficient to define it as "education for citizenship," without first revising our concepts, both of education and of citizenship. I think it forces the issue into its true light to define it as "education for virtue," or moral education, for such words come as something of a shock to educators who think and act almost unconsciously within the presuppositions of scientific materialism. If, with Rousseau or Eric Gill, we prefer to look at the means rather than the end, we can call it education in *things*, education in poetic experience, in practical activities. But I should say that such education is all part of the play way, of games education. "We should pass our lives," said Plato, "in the playing of games"; and by games he meant, as I have said on an earlier page, not only activities like baseball and cricket, but ritual, song and dance, all the activities we call art.

We shall re-define virtue and morality as we go along. Concepts like valour, purity, justice and wisdom, which were the typical virtues in Plato's world, may need re-definition in our world. But once we are in possession of them, once we are united in the exercise of such virtues, then I think it will be found that we have recovered that lost quality in living which I called *zest*. We shall so reform our industrial structure, the conditions of labor and production, that our daily work will once more be zestful, and the division which exists between work and play will largely disappear. And with its disappearance we shall have solved the problem of leisure. For there is no leisure problem in a healthy society: it is merely the time we reserve for rest, or meditation, or recreation, in a life which is otherwise fully occupied with creative activities, by which I mean simply making things, doing things. When what we do is "the exercise of human skill and imagination in *every* department of human work,"[4] then the distinctions between work and play, between art and industry, between vocation and recreation, between games and poetry—all these false distinctions disappear. Man becomes a whole man, and his way of life a continual celebration of his strength and imagination.

---

[4] Eric Gill, *Last Essays* (London, 1942), p. 56.

III

THE DISCIPLINE OF ART

IN A REMARKABLE PAMPHLET CALLED "Story of a School" which was published in 1949 by the Ministry of Education in London, the author, Mr. A. L. Stone, remarks quite casually that the qualities which were developed by the children in his school as a result of the methods he introduced might be described as interest, concentration and imagination. If we pause a little on those words—interest, concentration, imagination—we begin to realize that they are the key words in the whole process of education, from infancy to maturity. Without interest the child does not begin to learn; without concentration he is not capable of learning; and without imagination he is unable to make creative use of what he has learnt.

The experimental method introduced by Mr. Stone into a junior school in Birmingham, England, in an environment which the Ministry mildly describes as "discouraging," was the method we call "education through art," by which we mean, not finding a place of some sort for art in general education, but making art the basis of all teaching whatsoever. I wrote a book called *Education Through Art* to show how that idea might be justified in theory, but Mr. Stone proved the idea in practice. It was a demonstration of quite revolutionary significance. It is true that, as Mr. Stone says:

> . . . the approach we evolved in the school had nothing revolutionary in its nature. It was based on two elementary facts reiterated by education-ists throughout the ages. We tried to give the chil-dren opportunities to move and to express them-selves.

It was as simple as that, but the skill—the genius, I would say—lay in devising those opportunities. But they were devised, mainly in the form of play and drama, with all the arts as ancillary to these activities, and the result was not merely a reform in education, but a transformation of life itself.

Mr. Stone and his fellow teachers made many im-portant discoveries in the course of their experiment —discoveries that ought to be carefully considered by all educational psychologists. But their most im-portant discovery is summed up in one sentence: "We realised," writes Mr. Stone on the last page of his story, "that discipline was the outcome of the child's absorption in his experience and not a thing imposed by the teachers."

Discipline is, I suppose, a minatory word. Years of false discipline have filled us with images of canes and castor oil, police sergeants and sergeant-majors, all the dreary ritual of the barrack square and parade ground. How rarely do we remember that the word is derived from the same root as "disciple," a gentle word, full of reverence and devotion. The proper meaning of discipline is, indeed, "discipleship." When we get back to the original Latin meaning of the word, we find that it is identical with the meaning of our word teaching, a word which implies pointing out, showing, the relationship of master to pupil. Discipline is involved in that relationship, but I hope to show how different such discipline is from the discipline of the barrack square.

If we could restore the proper sense to the word discipline, then it might replace, in our discussions of education, the much-abused word freedom. "Freedom in education" has been one of our slogans, and most of us have probably made use of it at one time or another. But it is a cant phrase that covers much loose thinking and random experiment.

"Freedom" as a word stands for something very important, as I have suggested in Chapter I, but it is the end and not the means of education. It is a spiritual condition or mental state to which we attain only after long periods of training. It has nothing whatsoever to do with that laissez-faire attitude in education which so often goes by the name of freedom. "Live and let live" is a good motto among responsible adults, but it has no place in the school where life is a tender shoot, to be protected, shielded, guided, led into the light.

The application of theory is often impractical and reckless to an extent that would horrify the originators of theory, who in the present case were, for the most part, prim moralists. Even Rousseau, who has been held responsible for so much that has happened since the publication of *Emile*, was a moralist at heart, and, far from giving his pupils "freedom," proposed to tend them and train them with the earnest solicitude of a stockbreeder. Pestalozzi, the most effective of all these pioneers, was a great liberator on whose lips the most frequent words were order and morality!

However, it is not Rousseau and Pestalozzi who are nowadays invoked where freedom is the catchword, but rather Sigmund Freud and Wilhelm Reich. I am not sufficiently acquainted with Reich's theories of education to know whether they justify the idea of freedom at any price; but in Freud's case there is no doubt. A steady look into the horrifying depths of the unconscious had left him convinced that education must be severely repressive. It could be, of course—perhaps most often was—stupidly, clumsily repressive; but that repression of some kind is necessary was never doubted by Freud, who said, in a lecture I have already quoted at greater length:

> The function of education is to inhibit, forbid and suppress . . . The child has to learn to control its instincts. To grant it complete freedom, so that it obeys all its impulses without any restriction, is impossible. It would be a very instructive experiment for child psychologists, but it would make life impossible for the parents and would do serious damage to the children themselves, as would be seen partly at the time, and partly during subsequent years.[1]

At the same time Freud recognized the enormous danger of the process. The wrong kind, the wrong way, of suppression would lead inevitably to neurotic illness. So Freud looked for an "optimum" of education, an education that could steer between the Scylla of giving the instincts free play and the Charybdis of frustrating them. It is, he said, a question of finding out how much one may forbid, at which times and by what methods. Freud remained an authoritarian; but he naturally hoped that all authoritarians would acquire "a good grounding in psycho-analysis."

I think that it is an extraordinary limitation, not only in Freud, but in psychoanalytical theory in gen-

---

[1] *New Introductory Lectures on Psycho-analysis* (London, 1933), p. 191.

eral, that it has not been able to suggest an alternative
to authoritarian discipline in education—that it can
only talk helplessly of "not too little and not too
much." It recognizes the inevitable risks of methods
of suppression, but with a resigned shrug towards
Scylla and Charybdis accepts these risks—ignoring
the fact that the real problem is to circumnavigate
those metaphorical rocks.

I think we might state, in the first place, that any
solution of the problem must substitute for authoritarian suppression some influence or bias which will
allow the instincts to emerge, to be expressed, and
yet at the same time ensure that this free expansion
is not harmful to the individual or to society.

Psychoanalysis has given the name *sublimation* to a
process that might be confused with our aim. But
sublimation, if I understand Freud rightly, always involves a substitution for or modification of the original
impulses—a particular impulse (say the sexual) is
suppressed, and by way of compensation the individual
in question begins to climb mountains, or to spend
all his spare time tinkering with his car. But Freud
quite rightly saw no connection between this process
of substitutive satisfaction and the process of education. Sublimation may be a useful safety valve in a
community of people with over-inhibited instincts,
but it has no bearing on instincts that are not in-
hibited or that it is not desirable to inhibit. It is, we
might say with limited truth, an evasion of the issue.

There is a more constructive suggestion in Jung's theory of *individuation*. At first Jung's ideas on child education seem to be disappointing. Although he was very interested in the dreams of children (and particularly in his own dreams when a child), he never seems to have paid much attention to the drawings of children although, as I more than once pointed out to him, they are full of archetypal symbolism. There was a good reason in his psychology for this apparent neglect. Although he fully recognized "the extraordinary plasticity of the child's mind," he saw this as a danger rather than as an opportunity. Just because the young child is at the mercy of those who surround it, it would be safer to trust to the indirect influence of a good environment rather than to entrust such a sensitive organism to the well-meaning but ignorant interference of human agents. A policy of laissez-faire might be best until such time as the child could become conscious of its own needs and guide its own destiny.

Jung distinguished three kinds of education: (1) *Education through example,* of which he said, "this kind of education can proceed wholly unconsciously and is therefore the oldest and perhaps the most effective form of all";[2] (2) *collective education,* by which he meant "not necessarily education *en masse*

----

[2] This and subsequent quotations are taken from *The Collected Works of C. G. Jung: The Development of Personality,* vol. 17 trans. R. F. C. Hull (New York; London, 1954).

(as in schools), but education according to rules, principles and methods"; and (3) *individual education,* in which all rules, principles and systems "must be subordinated to the one purpose of bringing out the specific individuality of the pupil."

The guiding principle in all Jung's thoughts on education is that we can only correct what is in our consciousness; *what is unconscious remains unchanged.* But all environmental influences are unconscious.

> The first impressions of life are the strongest and most profound, even though they are unconscious—perhaps indeed for that very reason, for as long as they are unconscious they are not subject to change.

In the first stage of education the child is psychologically more or less identical with its environment, especially with its parents, and Jung (lecturing at the International Congress of Education at Heidelberg in 1925, the same Congress at which Martin Buber delivered his important lecture on the creative powers of the child)[3] did not hesitate to compare the child in this respect to primitive people for whose psychic peculiarities Lévy-Bruhl coined the term "participa-

---

[3] *Between Man and Man,* trans. Ronald Gregor Smith (London, 1947), pp. 83–103.

tion mystique." "In the last analysis," Jung declared, "all education rests on this fundamental fact of *psychic identity,* and in all cases the deciding factor is this seemingly *automatic contagion through example.*" But this being so, one might venture to suggest that Jung did not pay sufficient attention to those educators who stress the necessity of changing the child's environment—by social reforms which would alleviate parental anxiety, and by attention to the aesthetic quality of the physical environment.

As for what Jung called collective education (education according to rules and principles), here the danger is that in our desire to make the child a good citizen and a useful member of society, we tend to foster *collective values* at the expense of *individual uniqueness.* Such a "perfect paragon of educational rules" tends to feel insecure in all matters where individual judgments have to be made without recourse to the regulations. But Jung was careful to distinguish between individual uniqueness and individual idiosyncrasy. Jung tended to adopt the compromise position which holds that a general system of collective education (of the right kind) may be good enough for most children, but that beyond this conventional system there exists a superior form of education (the third realm of education as I call it in a later chapter) which Jung calls the third realm of education, namely *individual* education.

In applying this method, all rules, principles and systems must be subordinated to the one purpose of bringing out *the specific individuality of the pupil*. This aim is directly opposed to that of collective education, which seeks to level out and make uniform.

But then comes the paradox of Jung's theory of education—this third and most important kind of education cannot be applied to children!

The fact is that the high ideal of educating the personality is not for children: for what is usually meant by personality—a well-rounded psychic whole that is capable of resistance and abounding in energy—is an *adult* ideal. It is only in an age like ours, when the individual is unconscious of the problems of adult life, or—what is worse—when he consciously shirks them, that people could wish to foist this ideal on to childhood. I suspect our contemporary pedagogical and psychological enthusiasm for the child of dishonourable intentions: we talk about the child, but we should mean the child in the adult, for in every adult there lurks a child—an eternal child, something that is always becoming, is never completed, and calls for unceasing care, attention and education. That is the part of the human personality which wants to develop and become whole.

So in this way the process of individual education becomes identical with the wider process of the integration of the personality, which is the chief aim of Jung's psychology. "And it is not the child, but only the adult, who can achieve personality as the fruit of a full life directed to this end." An unattainable ideal, as Jung confesses, "but unattainability is no argument against the ideal, for ideals are only signposts, never the goal."

"Fidelity to the law of one's being" is another way of expressing the same educational ideal. A dangerous ideal, as Jung recognized, but a necessary ideal for the salvation of humanity, and all Jung's work might be conceived as a long propaedeutic effort to make the ideal a safe one. The conventions of collective education are not enough—they are soulless mechanisms that can never touch more than the routine of life.

> Creative life always stands outside convention. That is why, when the mere routine of life predominates in the form of convention and tradition, there is bound to be a destructive outbreak of creative energy. This outbreak is a catastrophe only when it is a mass phenomenon, but never in the individual who consciously submits to these higher powers and serves them with all his strength.

In the last year or two of his life Jung had become increasingly aware of the part which art had to play in the conscious control of these creative energies. In September 1960 he wrote a long letter to me in which he spoke of his passionate interest in modern art and of his desire to come to terms with its schizophrenic significance. Perhaps I may quote the most moving paragraph from this letter:

> The great problem of our time is the fact that we don't understand what is happening to the world. We are confronted with the darkness of our soul, the Unconscious. It sends up its dark and unrecognizable urges. It hollows out and hacks up the shapes of our culture and its historical dominants. We have no dominants any more, they are in the future. Our wishes are shifting, everything loses its certainty, even *sanctissima causalitas* has descended from the throne of the *axioma* and has become a mere field of probability. Who is the awe-inspiring guest who knocks at our door portentously? Fear precedes him, showing that ultimate values already flow towards him. Our hitherto believed values decay accordingly and our only certainty is, that the new world will be something different from what we were used to. If any of his ways will show some inclination to incarnate in a known shape, the creative artist will not trust it. He will say "thou art not what thou sayeth,"

and he will hollow them out and hack them up. That is where we are now. They have not yet learned to discriminate between their wilful mind and the objective manifestations of the Psyche. They have not yet learned to be objective with their own psyche, i.e. between the thing which you do and the thing that happens to you. . . . If the artist of today could only see what the psyche is spontaneously producing and what he as a consciousness is inventing, he would notice that the dream, for instance, or the object [through his psyche] is pronouncing a reality from which he will never escape, because nobody will ever transcend the structure of the psyche. We have simply got to listen [to] what the psyche spontaneously says to us. What the dream, which is not manufactured through us, says, is *just so*. Say it again as well as you can. *Quod Natura relinquit imperfectum, Ars perficit.*[4]

Consciousness and the unconscious, Jung recognized, do not make a unity when either is suppressed or damaged by the other. Both are aspects of life, and we must discover how to bring them to terms with one another.

This means at once open conflict and open collaboration. Yet, paradoxically, this is presumably

---

[4] The original text of Dr. Jung's letter is in English.

what human life should be. It is the old play of hammer and anvil: the suffering iron between them will in the end be shaped into an unbreakable whole, the individual.

Again, there is something like resignation in the attitude: the human personality is "shaped," but beneath blind hammer blows, roughly. And even so, Jung says, we are dealing with something unpredictable: "We do not know how and in what direction the budding personality will develop, and we have learned enough of nature and the reality of the world to be somewhat distrustful." If we have discarded the Christian belief in original sin, it is only to find ourselves saddled with an equally grim heritage—the lower depths of Freud's dynamic unconscious. Can we seriously contemplate a friendly compromise between reason and such potent devils? Well, concludes Jung, the risk must be run, if only by the bolder spirits:

> The development of personality from its germinal state to full consciousness is at once a charism and a curse. Its full result is the conscious and unavoidable separation of the single being from the undifferentiated and unconscious herd. This means isolation, and there is no more comforting word for it.

From this point of view, education would seem to be a process of leading the individual away from the group, whose instincts are mass instincts, evil and catastrophic. Our epoch, says Jung, calls for:

> . . . the liberating personality, for the one who distinguishes himself from the inescapable power of collectivity, thus freeing himself at least in a psychic way, and who lights a hopeful watch-fire announcing to others that at least *one* man has succeeded in escaping from the fateful identity with the group soul.

Jung does not see this achievement as one of education. The analyst may contribute to the process as overseer, and to that degree as teacher. But only to an audience of one unique person. That person must make the individual effort, and it will always be a strenuous effort.

> Only the man who is able *consciously* to affirm the power of the vocation confronting him from within becomes a personality. . . . The greatness and liberating effect of all genuine personality consists in this, that it subjects itself of free choice to its vocation and consciously translates into its own individual reality what would lead only to ruin if it were lived unconsciously by the group.

There is a further extension of Jung's psychology which I must mention, since it leads towards what I regard as the essential problem. Jung makes a distinction between "genuine" personality, or "unique" individuality, and what he calls the conscious personality, or *persona,* "which is a piece cut off, more or less arbitrarily, from the collective psyche," a mask which simulates individuality, "pretending to others and to itself that it is individual, whilst it simply plays a part in which the collective psyche speaks."[5] There is, that is to say, an *inner* individuality, and mediating between this and the collective psyche is an *outer* individuality. The process of individuation is therefore best described as a dissolution of the *persona,* a gradual merging of the mask into the real face behind it—as if the mask, which is of a conventional *type,* had gradually become transparent and revealed underneath the irregular, unique features of a human personality. Since education in general consists in the creation of a conventional type (the gentleman, the good citizen, the comrade), Jung's process of individuation is fundamentally a process opposed to the normal ideal of education—the Jungian "individual," we may conclude, is not likely to be either a perfect gentleman or a good comrade.

The danger in this process, if I understand it properly, would seem to lie in its isolating tendency. It would set up a condition of what another psychologist,

---

[5] "Two Essays on Analytical Psychology," *Collected Works,* vol. 7, s. 468 (London and New York, 1953), p. 276.

Trigant Burrow, has called *ditention*—that "mode of attention that tends to divert interest in the object to interest in oneself—in one's self-image and its secret gain."[6] Dr. Burrow is as contemptuous of the *persona* as is Jung; but he is far more alarmed by the dangers of autopathic (self-centred) thinking. We cannot divorce an individual from his organic inter-relations with his environment and with his social group without in effect severing *vital* communications. I share Trigant Burrow's belief that "the outstanding factor in the external symptomatology of neurosis is the cleavage between the individual and his environment." I am certain that the only explanation of the vagaries of "culture" is to be found in this factor, and I suspect that the same explanation accounts for the futility of modern education.

I would like to spend some time summarizing and propagating Dr. Burrow's theories, which I regard as one of the greatest contributions which America has made to modern psychology, but I should be involved in the use of an unfamiliar vocabulary, and should run the risk of misrepresenting the scientific formulation of some very contentious ideas. I must ask the reader to seek illumination in the Doctor's own works, particularly in the one entitled *The Neu-*

---

6 *The Neurosis of Man: An Introduction to a Science of Human Behaviour* (London and New York, 1949), p. 72. The complete text of this volume was subsequently included in *Science and Man's Behaviour* (New York: Philosophical Library, 1953).

rosis of Man. But Dr. Burrow's thesis is already embodied in the familiar allegory of the Fall of Man. He himself refers to this archetypal myth in the following terms:

> With the beginning of consciousness man was set at odds with himself and with his environment. Man first became conscious when he became a person—when he ate of the fruit of knowing and *knew* he was a person. In knowing he was a person, in becoming a separate subjective 'I,' man lost contact with the solidarity of his organism as a species; he lost contact with the very soil that had nourished him. His motivation as a total species in relation to the environment was now interrupted by the innovation of the symbol, of language or knowing. Through man's constant substitution of the symbol, or of separate, ulterior knowing, he himself became but a symbol. He became part of a separate and ulterior system of symbolic knowing. This was the genesis of man's partitive behaviour. This the rudiment of man's psychosis.

The significance of the allegory has never been in doubt. What man acquired at the Fall was "the knowledge of good and evil"—that is to say, a conscience, or super-ego as Freud calls it, liable to guilt or anxiety, a mind full of fear and separation—separation from the "one flesh," which had been shameless; separation from the rest of animal creation; and separation from the Garden of Eden, that is to say, from the environment of beneficent organic growth.

> Cursed is the ground for thy sake; in sorrow shalt thou eat of it all the days of thy life; thorns also and thistles shall it bring forth to thee. . . .

Such was to be the future pattern of a neurotic society.

To restore the Age of Innocence, though it has seemed the only worthwhile objective to mystics such as William Blake, will hardly be taken on as a compendious assignment by psychiatrists and educationists. But what, in all modesty, is to be our aim? To alleviate suffering, to ameliorate the conditions of human life, to indulge in wishful thinking, in escapist fantasies? All these alternatives are possible, but they scarcely touch the surface of our neurosis, which meanwhile finds expression in universal hatred, in catastrophic warfare, in frenzies that threaten the human race itself with destruction.

The most simple, direct and elementary affirmation of life, of the vital principle in our being, requires that we should make the effort to restore the Age of Innocence—or, if we must express the same ideal in a different phraseology, re-establish the human organism's primary unity of motivation and behaviour.

The essential dogma, hypothesis or fact—call it what you will according to your temperament— with which we set out on this enterprise states in Dr. Burrow's words that:

> The organism of man in its primary integral functioning is one and continuous with the consistent harmony of the physical world of matter and energy around him.

The deduction that follows is that "only as man's motivation or behaviour is consciously co-ordinated and at one with this harmonious principle operating within and about him" does man give to this principle "a consistent, intelligent, living acknowledgement."[7]

There is nothing strange in the principle thus cryptically formulated, or in the practical application of it here demanded. We find the same formula in early Chinese ethical teachings, above all in the *Tao-tê-ching;* in the pre-Socratic Greek thinkers; and then fearlessly and persistently applied in the philosophy of Plato. One might call this policy of discovering and then collaborating with the harmonic forces of the physical universe the basic precept of a universal wisdom; the difficulty has been to formulate the practical rules for the realization of such a law in daily life.

---

[7] *Neurosis of Man,* p. 166.

Plato failed to persuade his fellow Athenians or even the philosopher-kings of his own time to adopt his proposals. Subsequent philosophers have played with the same idea, but apart from Schiller none has dared to make it an integral part of ethical teaching. The reason is perhaps obvious. To retreat from self-consciousness is to abandon philosophy itself—religion too, all the symbolic systems by means of which man expresses his dualistic plight, his lack of animal faith, his existential dread.

We might begin our approach to the educational problem, then, with this simple but far-reaching question: Do we wish to increase or decrease man's sense of separateness, of existential aloneness and uniqueness? Would it not be better to seek means of increasing man's sense of belonging to the organic order, his sense of unity with the species, his unselfconscious acceptance of a human, and even a universal, oneness?

It is arguable that there is no choice at all—that mankind is committed to a disintegration into separate and mutually repellent "I-*personae*," and that the only mitigation of our despair is to be sought in authoritarian symbolism—the mutually repellent units being forced into a compact "pile" or prison, a universal church or a universal state. A "unity" of that kind is perfectly feasible, and the example we have before us in the U.S.S.R. (nominally as well as actually a *Union*) shows apparently that this kind of unity may be acceptable to millions of people. But even in Russia considerable emphasis is given, if only for propaganda, to compensatory elements of diversity—the diversity of local languages, customs and cultural products. It may be that in our democratic dread of any form of totalitarianism, we are neglecting to observe important aspects of the social experiment in Russia. There is nothing in the available evidence to suggest that the Russian people is any less free from neurosis than the people of Western Europe or the United States: if fear and suspicion are symptoms of neurosis, then the disease would seem to be universal. But the process of ridding a whole nation of a neurosis is obviously "long term," and scientific caution is the best attitude to adopt to such a situation.

At the same time I do not see how "unity" is to be achieved by an external agency of any kind. The unity of sheep driven into a fold by the shepherd and his dog is a unity for the sheep, but it leaves the shepherd outside. An all-embracing unity must be spontaneous, generated within the human species (or phylum). It must not depend on any artificially maintained control from outside.

The more one considers the problems of life—problems of society, of culture, of art and ethics—the more the conviction grows that the secret lies within the concept of *spontaneity*. This is a concept very difficult to reconcile with logic, with the scientific bias towards order and system. One cannot say that the concept has been ignored by modern philosophers: indeed, it is central to the metaphysics of Bergson, for example, and of Whitehead, to mention no others. But what can be established biologically, and then philosophically, still has to be translated into practice, and that is precisely our own problem—to describe and initiate a method of spontaneous development, of creative education.

Let us try and appreciate the difficulty of the task we have set ourselves. We begin with the proposition for which I think Bergson offered sufficient proof— that mobility or change is of the essence of reality— we are not part of a world of fixed definitions, of defined limits, destined to fit into its pattern. It is true, as Bergson admitted, that:

> Our mind, which seeks for solid points of support, has for its main function in the ordinary course of life that of representing *states* and *things*. . . . It substitutes for the continuous the discontinuous, for motion stability, for tendency in process of change fixed points marking a direction of change and tendency. This substitution is necessary to common-sense, to practical life, and even, in a certain degree . . . to positive science.[8]

---

[8] *Introduction to Metaphysics*, trans. T. E. Hulme (London, 1913), p. 56.

Bergson says elsewhere:

In this way, reality is ordered exactly to the degree that it satisfies our thought. . . . But the mind can go in two opposite ways. Sometimes it follows its natural direction: there is then progress in the form of tension, continuous creation, free activity. Sometimes it inverts it and this inversion . . . leads to extension . . . to geometrical mechanism.[9]

In both cases we say that there is *order*.

The order of the second kind may be defined as geometry, which is its extreme limit; more generally it is that kind of order that is concerned whenever a relation of necessary determination is found between causes and effects. It evolves ideas of inertia, of passivity, of automatism. As to the first kind of order, it oscillates no doubt around finality; and yet we cannot define it as finality, for it is sometimes above, sometimes below. In its highest form, it is more than finality, for of a free action or a work of art we may say that they show a perfect order, and yet they can only be expressed in terms of ideas approximately, and after the event. Life in its entirety, regarded as a creative evolution, is something

[9] *Creative Evolution,* trans. Arthur Mitchell (London, 1914), p. 235 ff.

analogous; it transcends finality, if we understand by finality the realization of an idea conceived or conceivable in advance . . . the first kind of order is that of the *vital* or of the *willed,* in opposition to the second, which is that of the *inert* or *automatic.* Common-sense instinctively distinguishes between the two kinds of order, at least in the extreme cases; instinctively, also, it brings them together. We say of astronomical phenomena that they manifest an admirable order, meaning by this that they can be foreseen mathematically. And we find an order no less admirable in a symphony of Beethoven, which is genius, originality, and therefore unforeseeability itself.

The vital is in the direction of the voluntary—that is the essential point to seize. I find a certain difficulty in Bergson's identification of the vital and the willed, for what is willed, in our general usage of the term, is not spontaneous. But Bergson's "will" is the *élan vital,* and therefore certainly spontaneity itself. The underlying notion is perhaps brought out in a more concrete sense by Whitehead's use of the word adventure in *Adventure of Ideas.* Even perfection, Whitehead points out, can be too static for the health and vitality of civilizations.

Even perfection will not bear the tedium of indefinite repetition. To sustain a civilization with the intensity of its first ardour requires more than learning. Adventure is essential, namely, the search for new perfections.[10]

"Not to rest too completely on any continual realization of the same perfection of type" is the wise advice he gives us. Spontaneity, originality of decision, belong to the essence of the life process.

We are still very noticeably in the realm of abstractions. I will descend with a bump into the typical nursery and the kindergarten to ask what is happening to that bundle of spontaneity, the human child. Would it not be true to say that in general it is being rendered *inert* and *automatic?* It is being taught to sit still, to regularize its habits of eating and digestion, to formalize its speech, to conventionalize its behaviour in a hundred ways. Now, all this may be done in an enlightened and intelligent manner—that is to say, in subtle ways that do not arouse the child's immediate antagonism. "To be a good boy" is as simple as "to be a good dog"; we may not put the piece of sugar on the boy's nose, but we put an equivalent reward in his imagination, and the reflexes, with time and patience, become equally automatic.

We call the result *discipline,* and it is another illustration of Bergson's second kind of order. It is a *state* of being or existence, an achieved perfection. As such it can be one of two things: perfection for per-

---

[10] *Adventure of Ideas* (New York, 1933), chap. XVII, s. V-VI.

fection's sake, a code of abstract ethical conduct; or perfection for the sake of society—that is, a perfect conformity to a traditional pattern.

The advantages of such conformity—one might even say its ethical rightness and aesthetic beauty—are so great as to make that form of education supremely attractive. In God's name, you might cry, what more do we want? And you would only be echoing the cry of Plato, for example, who admired the millennial conformity of Egyptian society, or of Aristotle, of Hobbes and Rousseau, indeed, of almost every great sociologist of the past, until we come to the critics of perfection of whom Vico was perhaps the first, as Whitehead is the last. Let us add, for such reinforcement as their names give, Schiller, Goethe, Nietzsche, Ibsen, Burckhardt, Bergson and Shaw. All in some degree have perceived that the achievement of perfection involves the withering of inspiration; that zest and vitality depend on a continuous renewal of inspiration.

That renewal must take place, I believe, in the child. At least, the possibility of renewal, an openness to inspiration, depends on a constitution of personality determined in the formative period of childhood. The splendours of a civilization are the creation of mature adults—that does not need to be affirmed; but the minds that animate those splendours are themselves the creation of a system of breeding, and

their power of animation depends on their fount
of inspiration. If that fount is sealed off in childhood,
whatever perfection is achieved is a dead perfection,
and doomed.

Something near perfection has existed in the past—
in Athens, in Byzantium, in China, even in medieval
Europe; but we cannot speak of perfection today, in
relation to our own civilization. Much less dare we
speak of inspiration, unless it is the inspiration of
evil. We are, in fact, the victims of a past perfection,
of a civilization that was incapable of renewing itself,
and has perished for lack of inspiration. The process
of disintegration has not been uniform—there has
been scientific adventure but no corresponding moral
adventure; practical adventure but no aesthetic adventure; or aesthetic adventure merely designed to
relieve a state of boredom. All that is intrinsical and
intense has been sacrificed to intellectual cults; the
thread of Ariadne ravelled in a series of repetitions
that began with the Classical revival, continued with
the Gothic revival, and ended in all the eclecticism
of the nineteenth century. These were symptoms of
an enfeebled inspiration, of an absence of spontaneity.
No amount of scientific invention could compensate
for such a spiritual poverty.

Let us return for a moment to a consideration of
the work of art, for in it not only Bergson and
Whitehead, but also Schiller and Nietzsche, have
recognized the presence of an apparent contradiction

—the co-existence in the same phenomenon of spontaneity and order, of vitality and discipline. There are several important observations to be made about this phenomenon. The most important is the one Coleridge first made—that the order or form in the work of art is not pre-fabricated and super-induced: in some sense it originates in the act of creation. It is an organic event, unfolding as naturally as the petals of the wild rose. It might be argued that the form of the rose is pre-determined and therefore super-induced, but that is to miss the essential point, which is that the rose grows into its particular form spontaneously, and is not aware of any restriction to that particular form. In the same way the artist is not aware of restriction to a particular form in creating a genuine work of art. The word genuine must be emphasized. Many a poet feels "restricted" when he is writing a sonnet; but that is precisely when he writes a bad sonnet. Every good poet is aware of the spontaneous accord between idea and form that signifies successful achievement. The question is: How does that accord come about?

No general answer to that question may be possible; but I would like to suggest that it depends on the possession of innate or acquired *skill*. I do not believe that there is any psychological difference of a fundamental kind between the skill of a dancer, of a poet, of a baseball or tennis player, of a painter, of a musician. Certain skills are confined to nervous and muscular co-ordinations; others take in a subtler and more extensive range of mental events—the difference between, for example, the repetition and the original composition of a violin sonata. These differences of degree are immensely important, but they do not affect our hypothesis—which is that creative freedom or spontaneity depends on unconscious discipline.

The formation of unconscious disciplines—that is perhaps not a very original definition of learning. But in pedagogical theory far too little emphasis has been given to the necessary unconsciousness of the acquisition. We learn the motions of a stroke, but muff the result because we *observe* the stroke, and muscles refuse to be co-ordinated by a conscious brain—they revolt against any form of dictation!

Certain rare instances of musical genius, and of other prodigious skills, show that the individual can be born with an unconscious discipline, but in general we must regard discipline as something to be acquired, and the business of education as the inculcation of such discipline. But how clumsily we approach this business! We are given this infinitely complicated, delicately co-ordinated mechanism which is the human child, and we begin to bang it about, box its ears, torture it in a thousand ways until it *obeys*. Obeys what? Well, in the first place, various restrictions on its instincts—*not* to make a mess, *not* to make a noise, *not* to inflict its natural desire for social activities on busy adults. Now, suppose we took even one of these primitive instincts—to make a mess, for example—and used that as a basis for spontaneous creative activity. We have already discovered that the child, before it can manage a pencil or a brush, can with immense pleasure dab its fingers into paint and transfer the colours, with some sense of purpose, to a clean sheet of paper. Where there is a sense of purpose, there are already the rudiments of a sense of discipline, already a co-ordination of muscular reflexes. Discipline has begun—has been born in the process of a primitive creative activity.

Similarly the instinct to make a noise—how easily this is satisfied with a drum beaten rhythmically, even if that drum is no more than an old tin can. Tin cans can be orchestrated with tin whistles and toy trumpets. With very little encouragement and guidance, the notion of melody emerges from a chaos of sound.

I believe that the whole development of the child can be built up as a sequence of such acquired disciplines. In development I include, not only the physical and expressive growth of the child from birth—the process to which psychoanalysts give the name "reality testing"—but also that knowledge of the external world and its cultural assets which is the normal aim of education. There is not a subject from simple arithmetic to calculus, from nature study to theoretical biology, from the writing of poetry to metaphysics, which cannot be acquired as an habitual discipline. In their integrated wholeness these disciplines constitute the Freudian super-ego, the dynamic conscience and the source of all moral sense.

Now comes a further significant point. Such disciplines do not isolate the individual—on the contrary, they create communion between the individual and a group. That was another of Mr. Stone's discoveries at Birmingham:

> Expression in the arts gives not only a natural approach to academic subjects but also a more confident basis for tackling the difficulties of social relationships.

The most effective disciplines are group disciplines —not the solo dancer, but the dancer in swing, in ballet, in folk dance; not the solo musician, but the player in a quartet or orchestra; not the solo painter, but the painter who is a member of a school, a studio, a movement. I admit that many arts have become lonely activities—the poet's art, for example —but that may be the explanation of their decline in popularity.

I am not suggesting that the poet or any other artist should merge his identity in the group: that is what Jung calls "the fateful identity with the group soul," and one cannot imagine the group soul producing any form of art higher than the ballad or community singing. Here, as always, it is a question of measure: of the right size of group, which is a size

the individual can grasp in its wholeness. To grasp
in its wholeness—that means to establish a relationship of tension and reciprocity. Not only must the
individual be aware of the wholeness of the group,
the group must be equally aware of the uniqueness
of the individual. We have such a relationship in the
team—the football team, the baseball team; we have
it in the orchestra and the corps de ballet. We *should*
have it in the social unit—we did have it in the feudal
organization of society, and we are recovering it in
certain forms of co-operative enterprise, such as
the *kvutza* in Israel. But above all we should have
this relationship in the school; for the discipline of
learning also requires co-operation. We learn best
when we teach one another, when we practise together.

The essence of co-operation is its spontaneity—how
often this was demonstrated in war! We must find
some other name for the automatic discipline of a
peace-time army, for the *inert* bondage of the em-
ployees in a factory or the clerks in a Government
office. In the one case discipline emerging spontaneously, as the necessary condition of an organic activity; in the other case, discipline imposed, as the
mechanical integration of discordant elements.

The discipline of art—obviously we must interpret
art in a wide sense, to include any constructive activity, any technique or skill. But such was the original
significance of the term, and the arts only became

dissociated from the normal activities of the community as they lost their integrity, their meaningful purpose for the community. Our first step in the schools should be to break down the isolation of art—to abolish it as a subject altogether if it is to be considered as a specialized activity, set apart. It should be the significant aspect, the *disciplined* aspect, of every activity; every subject should be one of the arts, and the aim of education should be to make us all masters of the arts. But to be a master of an art is to be also a member of a mystery—of one of the functional groups of an organic community.

IV

THE MORAL SIGNIFICANCE OF AESTHETIC EDUCATION

1. THE CONCEPT OF MORALITY

"THE WHOLE WORK OF EDUCATION and its *only* work may be summed up in the concept— morality." Such is the opening sentence of one of the decisive documents of the science of education: Johann Friedrich Herbart's essay "On the Aesthetic Revelation of the World as the Chief Work of Education." This essay, published in the year 1804 as an appendix to an exposition of Pestalozzi's methods of education, may be regarded as Herbart's first and profoundest attempt to give a scientific basis to the more empirical intuitions of the great Swiss teacher.

Everything, in Herbart's dogmatic statement, depends on the meaning we are to give to the word *morality*. Subject to an agreement on such a definition, I am going to assume that we can accept the view that morality is the whole and only aim of education. I fully realize that such an assumption, in the contemporary world, would not be universally accepted. To Plato, to Kant, to Rousseau and to Ruskin, the moral education of the citizen is the basis of their social philosophy; but there is little trace of such a philosophy in modern political programs. Morality is nowadays an uncomfortable concept, and is not the deliberate aim of any of the systems of education prevailing among the leading nations of the modern world. Those systems are more concerned with what is known as vocational training, and if it is sometimes admitted that "citizenship," for example, is also a vocation, this is taught rather as a blind obedience to an established authority than as any exercise involving the free will.

But let us, with the aid of Herbart and other unfashionable philosophers, proceed to make some definitions.

The will to be good and to do good—that is the simplest definition of what the world has always meant by morality. But even this simple definition needs a gloss, for unless we emphasize the word *will*, and insist on its presence as an active principle in the person, we fail both to understand the essential nature of morality and to distinguish it from a false conception of morality which all too easily takes its place.

There is in morality an inherent tendency to legalism. What we discover to be good and agree to be good, we like to formulate in rules and regulations, in precepts and commandments; and once this is done, once the Tables of the Law are engraved, then obedience is exacted. But then obedience is no longer moral. It may be submission based on fear, or a habit of conformity, or at best an intellectual assent to a rational code. But it is no longer what Herbart called a "taking place" *(Ereignis),* a natural event, an act of freedom, a "making" *(Machen)* which the pupil himself discovers when choosing the good and rejecting the bad.

Admittedly, obedience is of the essence of morality; but everything depends on what is obeyed and how it is obeyed. "But," says Herbart, "not every obedience to the first chance command is moral. The individual obeying must have examined, chosen, valued the command; that is, he himself must have raised it for himself to the level of a command. *The moral man commands himself.*"[1]

In our own time a similar distinction has been made by Bergson between a *social* and a *human* morality, between which, he says, there is a difference, not of degree, but of kind.[2] Social morality is a set of

---

[1] My quotations from Herbart are generally taken from *The Science of Education and the Aesthetic Revelation of the World,* trans. H. M. and E. Felkin (London, 1892).

[2] *Les deux sources de la morale et de la réligion* (Paris, 1932), p. 31.

habits, a pattern of behaviour, which is instilled by
a process of training and which is for the general
benefit of the existing structure of society; but human morality is a mystical sense of obligation produced by an *élan d'amour,* an emotional gesture, embracing the whole of humanity, and is itself one of
the highest manifestations in the individual of the
creative force of evolution. I shall not myself adopt
such a mystical explanation of this second type of
morality, but Bergson is undoubtedly right in distinguishing it clearly from social morality and in
giving it an altogether higher place in the scale of
human values.

But now let us ask, with Herbart, *what* is it that
the moral man commands himself? Such a question,
in Herbart's time, threw the philosophers into universal confusion. Kant, as is well known, by a species
of solipsism, invented the "categorical imperative."
Command yourself, he said, to be commanded by
your profoundest intuitions of the moral law. "Act on
maxims which can at the same time have for their
object themselves as universal laws of nature."
Other philosophers have given different answers—various theoretical or utilitarian concepts of virtue which
the individual must, paradoxically by an act of free
will, obey. But Herbart was the first to point out the
true state of affairs—that the moral man does not
command himself to do anything concrete or definite; that what exists is a certain predisposition of

the will, a certain readiness to act in any given situation. The categories of morality are dynamic, not static; they are inspired by a kind of primary energy, an original source of personal power—a power, that is to say, not of doing, but of *willing*. Obedience follows when this power is *engaged* by a concrete situation, when willing becomes action. For this reason Herbart calls this willing, which is real but not conditioned, an unconditioned *manifold*.

It is important to understand this subtle distinction, for the whole philosophy of education that follows hinges upon it. We must fully appreciate the fact that *obedience*, in this account of the moral disposition, does not relate to specific commandments, does not arise only with reference to particular circumstances; but is rather a creative self-command, controlling at will all manifestations of instinct and desire. In psychoanalytical terms we might correlate the unconditioned manifold of Herbart with the superego, to which Freud ascribes a function somewhat wider than the conscience—describing it as "something which enjoys a certain independence, pursues its own ends, and is independent of the ego as regards the energy at its disposal."[3]

If we have a clear realization of the indeterminate nature of this basic moral energy, which strictly speak-

3 *New Introductory Lectures,* trans. W. J. H. Sprott (London, 1933), p. 82.

ing becomes moral only as and when it is manifested in concrete situations, then we shall understand how impossible it is to suppose that such energy can be built up or formed by the intellect. It is to be infallible in its action, spontaneous in its application; but, as Herbart says, its composition[4] cannot be merely logical.

> It cannot be learned from a well-classified doctrine of morality; such a doctrine cools the will, and does not impel it. It requires much rather a partly poetical, partly pragmatic composition.

In a situation truly moral a person acts spontaneously. He is not commanded to act: he does not even command himself to act. It is not a question of *ought* or of *must:* there is no theoretical necessity to act in the way he does, and, as Herbart says, "to honour a command does not mean bowing to the inevitable." Herbart is very insistent on this point: the moral man, in his acts of obedience, is not conscious of being the owner of an inner store of feeling and life, is not conscious, as we would now say, of the existence and functioning of his super-ego. "He dare not appear to himself as giving the decisive sentence"—the first essential of morality is destroyed

---

[4] Herbart uses the word "construction." I suspect that a modern German philosopher would use the word *Gestalt,* and certainly something like "the good *Gestalt"* seems to be meant.

if in any sense *will* becomes the ground of *command* —if what happens is merely that one form of arbitrariness is put in the place of another. The moral man is intrinsically humble; he acts from necessity, but it is not a necessity which he can even desire to submit to the test of reason.

Though he does not act from rational necessity, or from legal or social necessity, nevertheless the moral man acts from a necessity of some kind; and so Herbart comes to the conclusion that, among all known necessities, the only one left for consideration is *aesthetic* necessity. Can it be that in his acts of goodness the moral man obeys an aesthetic necessity?

2. AESTHETIC JUDGMENT

In answering this question in the affirmative, Herbart was following the lead primarily of Plato, but more immediately of Schiller, whose *Letters on the Aesthetic Education of Man* had been published only a few years previously. He may also have been influenced by Schelling, in whose system of Transcendental Idealism the aesthetic activity is fundamental—the only link between the Ideal and the Real. But Herbart makes no mention of these precursors, and, indeed, his argument is so closely reasoned that it has no need of extraneous support.

His first point is that aesthetic judgment[5] is absolute—it speaks entirely without proof, without attempting to enforce its claims; it takes no account of inclinations: it arises on the clear presentation of its object and is then spontaneous. There are as many aesthetic judgments as there are objects inviting such judgment, and such judgments are not related to each other in any way so as to be logically deducible from one another. It is true that formal similarities can be discovered among various objects, and that these naturally lead to similar judgments. But these formal relations—harmony in music, for example—demand absolute or simple judgments—they do not explain or prove anything.

Before Herbart, already Leibniz and Kant had admitted the absolute but irrational nature of aesthetic judgment, and the *Critique of Judgment* must have been fresh in Herbart's mind. But Kant had never dared to make the simple correlation between the moral will and the aesthetic judgment which Herbart made the basis of his theory of moral education.

What Herbart perceived as necessary in any system of moral education—and his intuition at this point is

---

[5] "Judgment" is the customary translation of *Urteilskraft,* but it is a word which I do not find happily associated with the aesthetic experience. The German word more easily suggests "discernment" or "discrimination" than does the word judgment, and "recognition" is a word which perhaps fits the experience more closely still.

decisive—was a training which led to a natural state of self-discipline or inner control. What was required was some form of mental exercise, some practice of the will, which would give the will a perfected ability to make a choice, to exercise judgment, *to act*. We have already seen that such a choice should be free; that no element of calculation should enter into it, for he who calculates does not obey with his will, but discriminates with his reason.

Herbart found such a training in what he called "the aesthetic revelation of the world," and by this he meant an ever-expanding exercise, in the child, of aesthetic choice, aesthetic appreciation, and, perhaps, aesthetic creation. This, in effect, is what he says: Throw open the whole visible world to the child, arouse as many desires as you like, but don't let him be overwhelmed by them. Teach him to discriminate among the host of sensations which are aroused in him. Make him realize that he has within him an immeasurable store of will power which he can release when, where, and how necessity dictates. The necessity that dictates will be impersonal, a discipline determined by his aesthetic judgment, his innate taste. At this point Herbart becomes a little obscure, perhaps because he had no innate taste of his own. But I will give a paraphrase of his words: He imagines a boy to whom the world is a rich open circle filled with manifold life, and which this boy proceeds to

examine in all its parts.[6] What he can reach, he will
touch and investigate; the rest he will look at and
transfer to his mind. Herbart assumes that he will
take the measure of individuals, compare modes of
living and classes of society according to their splen-
dour, advantages and freedom. This seems to argue
a degree of reason in the boy which might be prig-
gish, but such a boy might be presumed, at least in
thought, to taste, to choose and to imitate among
the things he sees. Even if he makes no choice, but
just drifts in the pursuit of the pleasures of the moment, he will at any rate collect a store of keenly
observed phenomena, and he will gradually perceive
the necessity for discriminating among them. Herbart
assumes that "his concentrated reflection will grasp
all relations; the contrast of the ridiculous and the
seemly will determine his judgment as easily as his
behaviour." He will be predisposed to recognize and
value the beauty of goodness, and out of these
perceptions he will "prepare for himself a law,"
for he cannot do otherwise if he is free and has been
absorbed first in the aesthetic comprehension of the
world surrounding him, and not in the calculations of
egoism.

---

[6] Wordsworth, at almost the same moment, was giving his in-
comparable descriptions of the child's expanding universe. Cf. his
poem on the "Influence of Natural Objects in Calling Forth and
Strengthening the Imagination in Boyhood and Early Youth,"
composed 1799.

At this point I would take leave of Herbart, for when it comes to the question of how a general aesthetic revelation of the world must be planned by the educator, he has little to suggest beyond "early and wide reading of chosen classical poets," and, more vaguely, "the exercise of the pupils' perceptive power in the comprehension of works of art of all kinds." In this respect Herbart was hopelessly confined within the narrow concepts of art characteristic of his period. There may be good reason for feeding the imagination of the young boy (and Herbart was thinking of boys under ten) on the Homeric poems; that primitive world is one in which the child's imagination can accommodate itself. But there is more substance, and more realism, in Herbart's brief reference to the function of play in education. "The boy plays in real life," he says, "and it is by play that he realizes for himself his imaginings," a sentence that echoes Schiller's insistence on the significance of play *("Der Mensch spielt nur, wo er in voller Bedeutung des Wortes Mensch ist, und er ist nur da ganz Mensch, wo er spielt")*. And in the end Herbart returns to the concrete meaning of aesthetic revelation, as a developing knowledge or concept of nature of increasing sharpness of outline, as a system of forces and motions which, rigorously persistent in a course once begun, forms for us a type of law, and order, and sharply defined proportion. "Man," he says finely, stands in the midst of nature; himself a part of her, her power streaming through his innermost self, he answering external force with *his* own according to *his* method, *his* nature, first thinking, then willing, then working. Through his will goes the chain of nature.[7]

3. THE CHAIN OF NATURE

With these words Herbart aligns himself clearly with Plato, and it is in Plato that we find the most practical proposals for a system of aesthetic education, designed for the automatic guidance of the moral will. This system, which is outlined in the third book of the *Republic* and more thoroughly in the second book of the *Laws,* is based on the still sound presupposition that a child's first experiences in life are its feelings of pleasure and pain, and proceeds to the equally sound assumption that effective education is simply "learning to feel pleasure and pain about the right things." Plato then asks the same question as Herbart: What is there in the universe which is always concretely and objectively "right"—what is there that cannot fail to give pleasure to man? And he answers that question in the same positive but exclusive way: There is only aesthetic experience, and of all forms of aesthetic experience, the most direct

---

[7] Again, cf. Wordsworth, "The Recluse," ll. 110–51, and "Lines Composed a Few Miles Above Tintern Abbey," ll. 75–111.

in its action and infallible in effect is music. Plato therefore suggests that the whole education of the child should be pursued by aesthetic methods, above all by means of "choric art"—that is to say, the art of song accompanied by music and dance. Song is linked with poetry, and dance with gymnastics, and a natural expansion of education is envisaged which will finally include arithmetic, geometry and astronomy.

I think it is a mistake to pursue Plato's ideals too far into their practical details, which had in view a social economy very different from ours. Wrestling, for example, which had great significance for the Greeks in view of their methods of warfare, is not an educational aim of much importance in an age of atomic warfare. What is important to appreciate, and indeed to accept, is the basic principle—that aesthetic training is at the same time moral training; and to understand why Plato could put forward such an idea with complete seriousness and without any feeling of paradox. He was basing himself, of course, upon a doctrine generally accepted throughout the Hellenic world—the doctrine of universal harmony, of which Pythagoras had been the original exponent.[8]

---

[8] Werner Jaeger has *emphasized* the significance of this doctrine for the whole background of Greek thought:

All the marvellous principles of Greek thought—principles which have come to symbolize its most essential and indefeasible quality—were created in the sixth century. . . . One

This conception of a basic world harmony has persisted throughout the history of science and philosophy, and in a certain sense is, of course, the

of the most decisive advances in that process was the new investigation of the structure of music. The knowledge of the true nature of harmony and rhythm produced by that investigation would alone give Greek a permanent position in the history of civilization; for it affects almost every sphere of life. . . .

This harmony was expressed in the relation of the parts to the whole. But behind that harmony lay the mathematical conception of proportion, which, the Greeks believed, could be visually presented by geometrical figures. The harmony of the world is a complex idea: it means both musical harmony, in the sense of a beautiful concord between different sounds, and harmonious mathematical structure on rigid geometrical rules. The subsequent influence of the conception of harmony on all aspects of Greek life was immeasurably great. It affected not only sculpture and architecture, but poetry and rhetoric, religion and morality; all Greece came to realize that whatever a man made or did was governed by a severe rule, which like the rule of justice could not be transgressed with impunity—the rule of fitness or propriety. (πρέπον, ἁρμόττον.) Unless we trace the boundless working of this law in all spheres of Greek thought throughout classical and post-classical times, we cannot realize the powerful educative influence of the discovery of harmony. The conceptions of rhythm, relation, and of the mean are closely akin to it, or derive from it a more definite content. It is true not only of the idea of the cosmos, but also of harmony and rhythm, that it was necessary for Greece to discover their existence in "the nature of being" before she could employ them in the spiritual world, to find order and method in human life.

Paideia, the Ideals of Greek Culture, trans. Gilbert Highet, vol. 1 (3rd ed.; Cambridge, Mass., 1946; Oxford, 1946), pp. 164–5.

hypothesis upon which science itself proceeds. But whatever wider philosophical significance it may have, it is certain that the whole field of aesthetics, and particularly the concrete phenomena of art, is based upon harmony. Works of art, of whatever kind, give aesthetic pleasure when they illustrate universal laws of proportion and rhythm; that is, harmonic intervals of space or time. A work of art may do more than this—it may communicate intuitions or thoughts—but unless it has some basic harmonic form it is not a work of art. Such harmony need not necessarily be simple: indeed, as Bacon said, "there is no excellent beauty that hath not some strangeness in the proportion," a qualification, however, which Plato might have found difficult to admit.

The whole object of Plato's system of education is to produce a concord between art and behaviour, between the concreteness of beauty and the ethos of holiness or nobility. Plato, indeed, seems to have contemplated something as physical as a conditioned reflex. Here are some of the specific recommendations given in the *Laws:*

All young creatures are naturally full of fire, and can keep neither their limbs nor their voices quiet. They are perpetually breaking into disorderly cries and jumps, but whereas no other animal develops a sense of order of either kind, mankind forms a solitary exception. Order in movement is called *rhythm,* order in articulation —the blending of acute with grave—*pitch,* and the name of the combination of the two is *choric art.* (Bk. II, 664-5)

The choric art as a whole we found to be the same thing as the whole of education, and one half of the art, that which has to do with the voice, consists of rhythms and melodies. . . . And the part which deals with bodily movement has rhythm in common with the movements of the voice, but posture and gesticulation are proper to it, just as melody, on the other side, is to vocal movement. . . . The training of the voice to goodness, continued till it reaches the soul, we named, in a sense, music. . . . As for the training of the body—we spoke of it as the dancing of creatures at play—when the process culminates in goodness of body, let us call scientific bodily discipline with that purpose gymnastic. . . . This art . . . has its origin in the habitual leaping native to all living things, and in mankind . . . the acquisition of a sense of rhythm has generated dancing; since melody suggests and awakens consciousness of rhythm, the two in conjunction have given rise to the play of the choric dance.[9] (Bk. II, 672-3)

These quotations should suffice to show the practical nature of education in Plato's mature thought. It

[9] Trans. A. E. Taylor (London, 1934).

is not a question, as it is with us, of acquiring knowledge, of accumulating facts, of learning history or economics or physics. Education is primarily—that is to say, in its early stages—*physical culture;* it is concerned with the body, and *music* is that kind of physical culture which will produce mental excellence. Plato felt that there was a danger of making education too presumptuous: we must keep, he said, our seriousness for serious things—that is to say, our relationship to God—and as for the rest, all of us should fall in with our role and spend life in making our *play* as perfect as possible. Man at his best is God's plaything, and the best way of conducting our lives is to play so as to please God. "We should pass our lives," Plato concluded, "in the playing of games— *certain* games, that is, sacrifice, song and dance—in order to gain Heaven's grace. . . ."

4. *INSTINCTIVE OBEDIENCE*

These ideas of Plato have been echoed, nearer our time, in the Hellenic philosophy and "gay wisdom," as he would have it called, of Nietzsche. Though Nietzsche wrote a book on *The Future of Our Educational Institutions,* it is not there that we find his profoundest insight into the problem, but in later works which deal more generally with philosophical and ethical problems. Nietzsche realized that hitherto every "science of morals" had omitted the problem of morality itself—the pretensions of various philosophers "to give a basis to morality" proved merely, on examination, to be a learned form of good faith in prevailing morality. In other words, philosophers had never looked outside themselves, outside man, for a basis of morality. Like Plato, Nietzsche proposed that we should look to nature:

> . . . which teaches us to hate the *laisser-aller*, the too great freedom, and implants the need for limited horizons, for immediate duties—which teaches *the narrowing of perspectives.*

Everything in nature, he pointed out, which exhibits

> . . . freedom, elegance, boldness, dance and masterly certainty, which exists or has existed, whether it be in thought itself, or in administration, or in speaking and persuading, in art just as in conduct, has only developed by means of the tyranny of such arbitrary law.

And Nietzsche then points to the practice of art, where the free arranging, locating, disposing, and constructing in moments of inspiration are achieved only by the artist's obedience to a thousand laws, which, by their very rigidness and precision, defy all formulation by means of ideas. The essential thing, he says, is that:

... there should be long *obedience* in the same direction; and thereby results, and always has resulted in the long run, something which has made life worth living; for instance, virtue, art, music, dancing, reason, spirituality—anything whatever that is transfiguring, refined, foolish, or divine.[10]

Instinctive obedience to an aesthetic law—that might be given as Nietzsche's formula for a method of education which is, at the same time, the foundation of virtue or morality. It is, it will be seen, the same formula as Plato's and Herbart's; and though none of these philosophers presents exactly the same argument, or gives exactly the same emphasis to each phase of the educational process, all agree that the essential stages are these: (a) The recognition of the necessity of an order of discipline beyond morality itself; (b) the admission that the only necessity of this kind is aesthetic harmony; (c) the instinctive nature of the obedience to be achieved by moral education. I think the only further point which still needs to be rescued from current misconceptions concerns the nature of discipline. At the best, discipline is conceived as a method of achieving a certain end—firmness in danger, courage in adversity, endurance, social conformity, etc. It is even usual to consider it as no more than a systematic control of natural move-

10 *Beyond Good and Evil*, s. 188.

ments, as the reverse of liberty. We all know what, in scholastic circles, is meant by "a good disciplinarian"! Such a conception altogether misrepresents the true nature of discipline, especially in the context of education. Discipline from our point of view should be regarded, not as a means, but as an end. It is a branch of learning, and what is learnt is a positive ritual—a ritualistic control of the movements of the body and the field of attention. Group discipline, or social discipline, is what Plato called *sacrifice,* the performance of mass rituals. I am reminded that a philosopher with whom I was acquainted in my younger days would make an annual pilgrimage to the Aldershot Military Tattoo, which he regarded as the greatest work of art at that time available in England. We now have an art of ballet which is far more accessible to the general public, and which illustrates on a smaller scale the aesthetic value of disciplined actions. When Plato and Nietzsche speak of discipline, they have such types of coherent action in mind—they are certainly not thinking of a state of cowed obedience enforced by a master, rod in hand!

The value of such discipline lies in the freedom it confers. It is not only a mechanism which releases inspiration, as every writer or artist knows; it guarantees that the inspiration thus released shall flow in easy channels—that the mind, like the body, shall act with readiness, with economy, with precision. Athletic form, aesthetic form, ethical form—it is perfectly right that we should, in each context, use the word form. The form, in each case, is fundamentally identical. Plato further asserts that form in the physical sense ensures form in the spiritual or ethical sense; or, at least, that we can by training set up an inevitable association between physical and ethical form, the transition being effected by aesthetic exercises (by choric art, for example) which are partly physical and partly spiritual.

We should perhaps hesitate to use the word inevitable to describe the relationship between aesthetic education and moral virtue. Plato does clearly imply that once embarked on, his system of education inevitably leads to moral virtue. The element of choice, of free will, is present only when we decide to undergo such a training. It is possible that our modern research into the mechanism of the conditioned reflex lends support to Plato, but we must also try to reconcile our theory with the structure of the mental personality as revealed in psychoanalysis.

5. COMMON RITUALS

Unfortunately for our purposes psychoanalysis is a science of individual psychology, and except for Freud's essay on group psychology and the work of Trigant Burrow and his associates, it has so far made little attempt to deal positively with social morality.

The super-ego, or ego-ideal, which represents the moral principle in psychoanalysis, is nearly always treated as an isolated, personal structure. But the essence of morality, of course, is that it is universal—at any rate, that it is common to a specific group. Plato, for example, would never for a moment separate his concept of the virtuous man from his concept of the good citizen: the concepts are interchangeable.

In an important footnote to his essay on group psychology,[11] Freud admits that he has left part of the riddle of group formations untouched.

A far more fundamental and comprehensive psychological analysis would have to intervene at this point. A path leads by way of *imitation* to *empathy*, that is, to the comprehension of the mechanism by means of which we are enabled to take up any attitude at all towards another mental life. Moreover, there is still much to be explained in the manifestations of existing identifications. These result among other things in a person limiting his aggressiveness towards those with whom he has identified himself, and in his sparing them and giving them help.

Freud has previously explained that "identification," which is a technical term in psychoanalysis signifying the expression of an emotional tie with another per-

---

[11] *Group Psychology and the Analysis of the Ego,* trans. James Strachey (2nd ed., 1940), p. 70.

son, may arise with every new perception of a common quality shared with some other person who is not an object of the sexual instinct. Freud says:

> We already begin to divine that the mutual tie between the members of a group is in the nature of an identification of this kind, based upon an important emotional common quality; and *we may suspect* that this common quality lies in the nature of the tie with the leader. *Another suspicion* may tell us that we are far from having exhausted the problem of identification, and that we are faced by the process which psychology calls "empathy" *(Einfühlung),* and which plays the largest part in our understanding of what is inherently foreign to our ego in other people. But we shall here limit ourselves to the immediate emotional effects of identification, and shall leave to one side its significance for our intellectual life.[12]

It is precisely this significance of the process of identification for intellectual life that is our present concern. When Freud says that a path leads *by way of imitation to empathy,* he may or may not have been aware that he was indicating the path of art.[13]

---

[12] *Op. cit.,* pp. 65–6. (Author's italics.)

[13] Werner Jaeger points out (*op. cit.,* II, n. 86, 403) that in discussing the various types of poetry in the *Republic,* Plato uses *imitation* to mean "not copying some natural object or other, but

It is true that there is another path—identification with the leader—the totalitarian path in which there is no empathic relationship with other people, but only a blind obedience to one command. But that is not what we mean by morality: morality is essentially mutuality, the sharing of a common ideal. And the process by which we are induced to share a common ideal is none other than that indicated by Freud—the creation of an empathic relationship with our fellow citizens by means of common rituals, by means of the imitation of the same patterns—by meeting, as it were, in the common form or quality of the universally valid work of art.

From this psychological point of view the social function of art takes on an additional importance: it saves us from identification with a leader; it excludes the tyranny of the person; it unites us in the impersonal beauty of art.

I am willing to admit that art, in taking on such an important role in the educational and social development of mankind, must itself be modified. It is too often a wayward, partial, even perverse expression of universal harmony. It is too often but an expression of personal fantasies, of egoistic and aggressive impulses. It is prostituted to purposes which destroy its

the process by which the poet or actor assimilates himself (ὁμοιοῦν ἑαυτόν) to the person whom he is portraying, and thereby extinguishes his own personality for the time being." This is an accurate description of the process of *empathy*.

aesthetic nature. Our whole conception of art will have to be at once enlarged and purified. Plato recognized that necessity, and had elaborate schemes for its control and for the establishment of irrefutable canons of art. But control and censorship lead to the old danger of blind obedience, of will-less conformity. The perfection of art must arise from its practice—from the discipline of tools and materials, of form and function. For that reason we must give priority in our education to all forms of aesthetic activity, for in the course of making beautiful things there will take place a crystallization of the emotions into patterns that are the moulds of virtue. Such patterns are in effect social patterns, the patterns assumed by human relationships, and their harmony is part of the universal harmony, made manifest in life no less than in art.

V

THE REDEMPTION OF THE ROBOT

THE "ROBOT" WAS A satirical figure invented by the Czech dramatist Karel Capek more than forty years ago (in 1920) and maybe he is no longer an appropriate symbol for an age of automation. Capek saw man transformed into a machine: we see machines transformed into men. Man has been, or will be, eliminated from all productive processes. The machine not only produces, but computes, directs or determines qualities and quantities; as a controlling intelligence it is swifter and more accurate than the human brain. What then remains for man? What motives can now give meaning to his existence, and prevent the decay of his specifically human faculties?

The reader will be able to anticipate the answer I am going to give to these questions. I am going to say that man must become an artist and fill his new-found leisure with creative activity. But if the machine is to supply all his needs, what shall he create? Even pictures can now be painted by

machines, and music is independent of human instru-
mentation. More and more in our advanced technological communities, man will exist in a timeless,
motionless void. In this void the senses will atrophy
and what must emerge is something either less or
more than human.

In our despair we already fall back on that universal panacea, education. Since we shall no longer
need universal education of a practical or vocational
kind, we shall demand an education for leisure. Art is
cast for the role of redemptor. But is this its proper
function? Is education even the proper word for a
process that must be concerned with the adult rather
than the child?

I have in the past written and spoken often enough
about the place of the arts in education, and all I
have said has been based on the assumption that
we are concerned with a growing shoot that will respond as it grows to external influences and disci-
plinary activities. It seems to me that we are ap-
proaching an entirely different problem if growth has
come to an end and the object of our attention is no
longer tender and labile, but tough and settled in its
ways, an adult who has already found his place in the
world. Education in such circumstances is no longer
the appropriate term: what we must effect may well
be a transformation.

The concept of adult education is not new. As a
movement it dates back to the foundation in the early

part of the last century of various "mechanics in-stitutes" in the industrial regions of Great Britain. The traditional point of view, the point of view that in-spired the movement at its inception, held that its purpose was "to open up the great world of values, religion, literature, art, philosophy, history, even sci-ence, to those members of the community who, for one reason or another, have not hitherto had the op-portunity to share in the cultural wealth of man-kind."

Such a point of view belongs to an age when educa-tion was still a privilege of the wealthier classes. Now that education is universal, and that its benefits at least in intention are open to all who are fitted to make good use of them, a somewhat different view of the purpose of adult education has become necessary. It is no longer a question of giving the poor and ig-norant access to the cultural wealth of mankind. Since they already have all that wealth on their doorsteps, or at least on their television screens, it is now a ques-tion of *interpreting* that wealth to people not capa-ble of sorting it out for themselves. The simple task of imparting knowledge has been replaced by the much more difficult and dubious intention of creating values.

Sir Eric Ashby, one of our leading authorities on education in England, has suggested that a new in-terpretation of the humanities is now desirable. He would discard what he calls the "dated" concept of scientific humanism, which assumes that there is a contradiction between humanism and science which must be resolved. Like Lord Snow, he would get rid of this tiresome division between the humanities and the sciences and seek to establish one comprehensive culture acceptable alike to poets and physicists, to architects and biologists. Since we are entering a civilization of experts and technicians, the humanism appropriate to such a civilization, he suggests, must be one that confers values on the automatic factory and the aeroplane and the television and even the popular press: it must have something to offer the sort of man who a century ago could neither read nor write (but who was touched by contemporary culture all the same) and who now reads only the popular press and listens to broadcast programmes. He called this new humanism *technological* humanism.

It will be seen presently that I am largely in agreement with Sir Eric Ashby, though on this occasion I would not press the distinction he makes between science and technology. I have always been under the impression that technology was applied science, and in the actual examples which Sir Eric gave of the contents of two ideal courses of adult education in an era of technological humanism, it seems to me that nine tenths of the subject matter was what we would normally describe as scientific (and Sir Eric himself uses the terms "scientific method" and "scientific principles") and that the other tenth was merely a concession to the humanist's "great world of values." The weakest point in his exposition of technological humanism is unconsciously exposed in an addendum to his proposals—"Throughout these courses," adds Sir Eric, "students should have constant practice in the writing of simple English, especially descriptive writing about facts; and the courses should be taught historically rather than experimentally."

We must agree that all our efforts will be vain unless we adapt our methods of education to the kind of civilization we must inevitably live in, which means in effect teaching a subject from a central core of interest. But the writing of English, too, is a technique, based on principles no less scientific than those involved in the manufacture of refrigerators or "the 60-watt lamp." If we are to teach adults to write good English, the core of interest must be right there, in the writing of good English. Good English is good technology: good semantics; good technology functions through good English.

In an aside which invoked my name, Sir Eric expressed what I take to be the vital truth of the situation: "The establishment of standards of taste," he said, "is an essential ingredient of technology." In other words the arts have a function in a technological civilization; they are not an addendum, an optional "extra": they are an "essential ingredient" of technology, the values, presumably, that must be "fed into" the computing machine.

It is an unconscious assumption of almost all who discuss this subject that while in the course of this century we have entered into a new type of civilization, a technological civilization that has nothing in common with preceding civilizations, our cultural values have meanwhile remained static. The changes that have taken place, which are obvious, are described as decadent if in the sphere of morals, and as degenerate or schizophrenic if in the sphere of the arts. I am not concerned with morals for the moment, though my general assumption would be that however much moral habits may have changed, human nature is basically as good or as bad as it ever was. But in the arts—in our whole conception of the purposes and scope of the arts—a revolution has taken place in the past fifty years which is just as fundamental as the technological revolution, and which if accepted would make our task of integrating the arts into an era of technological humanism much simpler, much more effective. For the new conception of art is at the core of any technological method of production: it is the element of value in any formative process.

The new conception of art is sometimes called *formalism*, usually by those who wish to denigrate it. Personally, I have no objection to the term, which is closely descriptive, and which contrasts perfectly

with the opposed conception of art, which is humanistic.

The revolt against the exclusively humanistic conception of art has been long in gestation, but it first
comes into visible existence in the painting of Cézanne, and Cézanne's fundamental importance in the
history of this revolution is due precisely to the fact
that he was the first who dared assert that the purpose
of art is not to express an ideal, whether religious
or moral or humanistic, but simply to be humble
before nature, and to render the forms which close
observation could disentangle from vague visual impressions. The consequences of this peculiar kind of
honesty were hardly such as Cézanne himself would
have expected. First came cubism, and then a gradual
purification of form which reached its logical conclusion in the abstract or non-figurative art of Piet
Mondrian or Ben Nicholson. This formalist type of
art is now widespread among artists in every medium,
and whether you like it or not, like technology it has
come to stay.

It is not my present purpose to explain or defend
a formalist conception of art, but I would like to
emphasize the universality of the phenomenon. It is
not confined to the plastic arts: it is a philosophical
attitude that finds expression not only in painting and
sculpture, but also most obviously in the basic principles of modern architecture and in those branches of
technology such as aircraft production which have

not had their "standards of taste" bedevilled by ir-
relevant humanistic considerations. So far from technology being the enemy of art, I would rather go
to the other extreme and say that it has shown itself
capable of producing works which in absolute aesthetic value rival the Greek temple or the Gothic cathedral.
Some of these works are as anonymous as the Gothic
cathedral, but where we can name a designer, such
as Sir Geoffrey de Havilland, I do not hesitate to put
him in the same class as the architects of our great
cathedrals.

A correspondence would seem to exist, therefore,
between the spirit of modern art and the needs of
modern technology. Can we assume that the salvation of our civilization lies in this happy coincidence?
If civilization were only a question of form, the
answer might be affirmative, but can we make that
assumption? A sense of form seems to be an abstract and impoverished substitute for those noble
ideals of chivalry, of loyalty, of service and sacrifice
that have inspired the great civilizations of the past.
But we must not make the mistake of assuming that
form, however abstract or absolute, is necessarily inhuman. Form can be organic, and we have noted that
Cézanne assiduously searched for form in nature,
even in the human figure. Ruskin once observed that
"all beautiful lines are drawn under mathematical laws
organically transgressed." Form, we can therefore
say, need not be mathematical, in the strict sense of

the word. A de Havilland or a Boeing aircraft embodies forms similar to those organically evolved by birds and fishes: forms moulded by vital energies seeking structures adapted to a fluid medium like air or water. Man, in evolving his machines, is seeking analogous structures. An emphasis on form, therefore, although it may be anti-humanistic in the conventional sense of post-Renaissance humanism, is not an emphasis on faculties outside human experience, human perception, or human emotion. On the contrary, we may argue that the perception of the form beneath appearance is one of the highest functions of the human mind.

There is, however, a more serious objection to be answered. We speak of a technological civilization, and we are apt to visualize it in the terms of the typical productions of this civilization. It is assumed that the kind of people we have to educate in a technological age are productive workers—electronic engineers or aircraft designers. But productive craftsmen of this type represent but a small proportion of a technological society. Apart from the managerial and bureaucratic grades, there is a rank and file of unskilled labour that never have the chance to produce anything tangible—who are occupied in shifting things about, removing débris, and generally acting as intermediaries between those who produce and those who consume. This amorphous proletariat, who will be rendered redundant by automation, should be our main concern in any revision of our concept of adult education, and it would be as well if we would bear them in mind as we proceed with our discussion. We cannot avoid what is one of the central problems of our civilization and perhaps the prime source of its cultural weakness: the alienation of at least half the community from any practical skills, from concrete formative activities of any kind.

Our task, therefore, is twofold: to develop the aesthetic factors in technological planning and production, and to provide an aesthetic education for those who are no longer pursuing a technological vocation. Different methods of teaching will be necessary, though they have a common end in view, which is to establish the foundations of a new culture.

All attempts to effect social changes by educational methods are subject to one almost insuperable difficulty—the fact that we, the adult majority in the community, already consider ourselves educated. Only in rare cases are we willing to submit ourselves to a process of re-education. But even granted a willingness to submit ourselves to a process of re-education, there remain psychological factors, ingrained modes of response, or, more likely, a petrifaction of the very organs of response, which must be met by special measures, special techniques of teaching. These are the factors represented by the word adult.

Let me now recall to you the specific function of art in human life. It is a primary activity concerned with giving expression to our feelings and intuitions. By "expression" in this context we mean a physical form that we can perceive and apprehend. Art is the elemental language of communication, articulating the formless flux of sensible experience. It is a product of what Coleridge called "the shaping spirit of imagination." Croce said that works of art are passions brought to expressive shape. There is always this notion of a shaping of a formless flux of feeling, and this shaping of feeling is an activity that must be set in motion before the other specific functions of the mind—reason, desire or will—can proceed to their secondary task.

The artistic activity belongs essentially to the formative stages of a civilization, but a civilization is renewed and revitalized by the continuance of the process—by the recurrent injection of new visual images and new expressive shapes into the language and imagination of a race of men. Such is the basic biological and social function of art, and it is a function that is vitally necessary at the formative stages of a new civilization.

This process of renewal in an already established civilization is performed by the artists, and that is why the vitality of a civilization always depends on the free functioning of the aesthetic process. That is why a civilization without art perishes, and why a technological civilization will perish unless it can provide an outlet, or rather an inlet, for the shaping spirit of the imagination.

The inlet is situated in the mind of the individual, and we may say that at birth and throughout childhood it is wide open. But it gradually silts up with the dust of our practical activities, with the verbal mucus excreted by the rationalizing mind until, long before the individual becomes an adult, he is deaf and blind to all sensitive experiences, incapable of bringing new passions to expressive shape. We begin our task, therefore, with an individual whose aesthetic faculty is already atrophied, and our first task is to reanimate dead nerves, to reopen the doors of perception.

Of necessity this kind of "brain-washing" must be the prelude to any kind of art education for adults, but it is a stage of education that presents enormous difficulties, and for which very little experimental work has been done. But the little that has been done is very significant, so I will give some account of it.

There is first of all the large-scale experiment that was conducted at Weimar and Dessau in Germany between 1919 and 1928. Gropius's Bauhaus was essentially an experiment in adult education: the students were from seventeen to forty years old, most of them in their early twenties; half of them were ex-servicemen from the First World War. In establishing this experimental school Gropius's first step was to seek the co-operation of Johannes Itten, a teacher he had met in Vienna in 1918 whose theory of education had greatly impressed him. Itten had elaborated certain basic principles of teaching design, the purpose of which was to release the creative powers of the student. He began from the assumption that these powers were latent—either suppressed or atrophied—so the student was required in the first place to make a detailed study of materials, of the *nature* of materials, their physical structure, their colours and contrasted textures. Drawing from nature proceeded at the same time, to teach the pupil the principles of organic growth and configuration. Then, with a sensuous grasp of the nature of materials, and a knowledge of the functional forms evolved by nature, the student could begin to create his own significant forms. To quote Gropius's description of this preliminary course:

Concentration on any particular stylistic movement is studiously avoided. Observation and representation—with the intention of showing the desired identity of Form and Content—define the limits of the preliminary course. Its chief function is *to liberate the individual by breaking down conventional patterns of thought in order to make way for personal experiences and discoveries which will enable him to see his own potentialities and limitations.* For this reason collective work is not essential in the preliminary course. Both subjective and objective observation will be cultivated: both the system of ab-

stract laws and the interpretation of objective
matter.

Above all else, the discovery and proper valu-
ation of the individual's means of expression
shall be sought out.[1]

The detailed history of that experiment has been
written by Gropius himself and by others, and there
is perhaps only one aspect of it that I need emphasize now—it was a workshop education. That is to
say, it began with a full recognition of the technological basis of our civilization. The Bauhaus sought
to end the disastrous separation of the fine arts and
the practical crafts; students were taught independently by a master who was a craftsman and by a
master who was an artist. By this double training,
this co-ordinated instruction, it was intended to bring
into existence a new type of creative worker who
would be a functional unit in our technological civilization. It was recognized that out of this system
of training a minority would emerge who would
undertake independent research and experiment. These
would be the artists of a new age, the few excep-
tionally gifted ones "who will suffer no limits to their
activity."

The Bauhaus still remains the prototype of art

---

[1] *Bauhaus 1919–1928* eds. Herbert Bayer, Walter and Ise
Gropius (London, 1939), p. 26.

education in a technological civilization and it is only a fundamentally stupid conservatism that has retarded the development of the idea throughout the world, with disastrous effects on the international status of industrial design and technological efficiency.

Bauhaus education was essentially an education for adults, or at any rate for what we call post-graduate students. But it was not specially or specifically designed for the "adult" in our present sociological sense of the term, least of all for the displaced and disoriented robot. The adult in this sense presents a special problem because his sensibility, which is the aspect of personality that has to be trained in art education, is already atrophied. When I use the word atrophied I imply that his sensibility was once alive, and fundamental to all I have to say on this subject is the belief, based on the evidence of the activities of children and primitive peoples, that "every healthy man has a deep capacity for bringing to development the creative energies found in his nature, if he is deeply interested in his work." I use the words of Moholy-Nagy, one of the great teachers thrown up by the Bauhaus, who went on to say:

> Everyone is equipped by nature to receive and assimilate sensory experiences. Everyone is sensitive to tones and colours, has sure touch and space reactions, etc. This means that by nature

everyone is able to participate in all the pleasures of sensory experiences, that any healthy man can also become a musician, painter, sculptor, architect, just as when he speaks he is a "speaker." That is, he can give form to his reactions in any material. . . . The truth of this statement is evidenced in actual life: in a perilous situation or in moments of inspiration conventions and inhibitions of the daily routine are broken through, and the individual often reaches a plane of achievement otherwise not expected.[2]

I believe I was the first to give as an example of this spontaneous outbreak of artistic achievement the noble speech which Vanzetti, a poor ignorant cobbler, made when condemned to death for a crime he had not committed.[3] We all know that such spontaneous utterances of great beauty or nobility, exceptional as they may be in our normal lives, occur frequently in moments of stress. This formative and expressive energy lies dormant in every human psyche: and this is the energy that has to be released and geared to the functional activities of a technological civilization, in order to give that civilization a vital and progressive purpose. Such is the task of education, and, in particular, of adult education.

Now let me pass to some further experiments in

---

[2] *The New Vision* (London, 1939), p. 15.
[3] *English Prose Style* (London, 1928).

the art education of adults. In a remarkable book which should be "required reading" for everyone interested in the problems of adult education, Professor Henry Schaeffer-Simmern of the University of California has described a series of experiments in creative redemption which he carried out between 1939 and 1943 with four groups of people. The first was a group of mental defectives in a public institution of both sexes, their ages ranging from 11 to 35. The second experiment was with a group of delinquent youths, ages from 17 to 22. These two groups do not concern us directly, though the evidence is generally relevant. The third experiment was with a small group of refugees of various occupations, their ages ranging from 12 to 43; one was a physiotherapist of thirty. The fourth experiment was with a group of business people, their ages ranging from 27 to 54.

The detailed account of each case history is fascinating, but I have time only to recount Professor Schaeffer-Simmern's general conclusions as they relate to normal adults. However, I might say incidentally that the conclusions as they relate to abnormal individuals, mental defectives and delinquents are of the greatest educational and therapeutic interest.

The normal business and professional people in these groups began by being embarrassed because their first efforts were so "poor." Professor Schaeffer-Simmern tells us that:

Discussions threw light upon the fact that what
they had just produced looked childish because
their creative ability had never been developed
beyond the stages of childhood. But in so far
as the first results truly reflected their genuine
stage of artistic conceiving—primitive though it
appeared—a natural foundation was laid from
which development could take place. . . . With
their increasing power of visual discrimination
the students revealed a growing ability to produce
creative configuration. . . . With growing maturity in their pictorial results—that is, with the
attainment of a more complex visual order—
greater concentration of all forces was required and the working processes inevitably
slackened. It soon became obvious how creative
work adequately suited to the mental stage of its
producer can call forth unexpected powers. To
these "laymen" life seemed vitally enriched.
They experienced the rare pleasure of creation.

Professor Schaeffer-Simmern also relates that these
adults—as frequently stated by themselves—gradually
became conscious of:

. . . a unique cultivation of disciplined feeling and
thinking, of an intimate coordination of mind,
eye and hand, as well as manual skill. They felt
the formative effect which genuine artistic activity
had upon them as assisting towards a more
harmonized, more balanced personality.

And, more importantly, he points out that:

> . . . the spontaneous critical judgment which
> mainly caused the organic development of these
> students' artistic abilities was gradually applied,
> also, to observation of their environment. They
> became seriously aware of the fact that the
> greater part of their surrounding world did not
> possess that basic visual order which was the
> decisive quality of their own achievements. The
> deformed shapes of buildings, the utterly incoher-
> ent architectural planning of streets and squares,
> previously ignored by most of them, attracted
> their attention more and more. Simultaneously,
> they also became sensitive to the formless objects,
> the cheap as well as the expensive, displayed in
> shop windows. Instead of giving them visual satis-
> faction, such as they derived from the outcome
> of their well-organized artistic works, the mis-
> shapen objects aroused in them feelings of irrita-
> tion.[4]

Professor Schaeffer-Simmern's experiments did not
extend to the industrial arts, but the relevance of
the experiments to our technological civilization is
obvious: the demonstration justifies the assumption
that a form of visual cognition exists in man and
can be concretely realized in the work of art. Further,

---

[4] *The Unfolding of Artistic Activity* (Berkeley, 1950), pp.
194–7.

these experiments show that from the beginning artistic activity is autonomous, that is to say, independent of conceptual calculation and abstract thinking, a sensuous construction or "visual thinking," the elements of which are relationships of form.

One has to follow the experiments through, stage by stage, as described and illustrated in Professor Schaeffer-Simmern's book, to appreciate the revolution that occurred in the minds and lives of these people. Just as the drawings and paintings evolved from crude incompetent scribbles to skilful and expressive works of art, so life itself gradually became richer—richer in observation and experience, in satisfaction and self-confidence. In the words of one of these adults:

> As I developed a richer inner world I became critically aware of the outer world. Difficult as it is to describe the effect of this double enrichment on my personality, I can definitely say I am more fully awake to my surroundings, more fully alive. Multiply this effect on one average individual by only a small fraction of the population, and the social implications of artistic activity seem clearly self-evident.[5]

There is one further experiment I must refer to, the full account of which appeared in a book entitled *On*

---

[5] *Op. cit.*, p. 175.

Not Being Able to Paint, by Joanna Field.[6] This pen
name covers the identity of a practising psycho-
analyst, Dr. Marion Milner, and the experiment she
conducted was on herself. Since childhood she had
been interested in learning how to paint, but the
efforts had always tended to peter out "in a maze of
uncertainties about what a painter is really trying
to do." She began her experiment without any definite
purpose in mind—in fact, she discovered the important truth that *activity creates purpose,* and that the
secret of the creative process in the arts is a free interplay of differences—that the artist, "by embodying
the experience of illusion, provides the essential basis
for realising, making real, for feeling as well as
for knowing, the external world." The work of art,
she discovered, is essentially a fusion of an external
reality, based on perception, and an internal reality,
experienced as feeling. The work of art is an intuitive
image that acts as a bridge between lived experience
and logical thought, and as such has wide implications
for education.

Dr. Milner does not describe these implications in
any detail, for that is not the purpose of her book.
Its significance, from our present point of view, is
that it offers a solution to the problem of dormant
or atrophied sensibility which is the main difficulty
in teaching art to adults—"the kind of problem

---

[6] London (Heinemann Education Series), 1950.

that the over-introverted child is struggling with; and also, incidentally, what the over-introverted child is running away from." If this problem is not dealt with in the education of the child, we are left with an adult who has virtually to be psychoanalyzed before he can take part in creative activities of any kind. Luckily, as Dr. Milner demonstrates, the pursuit of the activities of art is in itself a process of self-analysis:

> The material in which the artist in us is trying to create is basically the raw stuff of human impulses. . . . In fact art creates nature, including human nature.

The experiments that I have been describing may seem to be too personal and only indirectly concerned with the immense social problem that confronts our technological civilization. Sir Eric Ashby has warned us that an emphasis on personal education, such as we get in the grammar schools and the art faculties of universities, is not consistent with the present crisis in our civilization. I am inclined to agree with him but not for the reasons he has in mind. He wants a technological humanism instead of a classical humanism, or whatever kind of humanism may be taught in our schools and universities. But humanism, by which is always meant a retrospective or synoptic vision of human knowledge, is not the answer to our problem, which is a problem of creating motives rather than of appreciating values —indeed, simply a problem of giving occupation to disused faculties. I am not satisfied even with Professor Schaeffer-Simmern's presentation of the problem, for he sees in artistic activities merely a compensation for the inadequacies of "the present highly industrialized . . . and mechanized civilization, in which [he says] more than ever, man needs an equalizing force for the development of his whole being." If this point of view implies that an artistic culture is in some sense inevitably divorced from the economic processes that supply our daily needs, then I venture to repeat a phrase which I have used as the title of one of my books, recently republished in the United States—to hell with such a culture![7]

There are two opposed dangers in any approach to art education of the kind we are considering. One is represented by the word *amateurism,* the other by the word *professionalism.* A state of war may be said to exist between the extreme factions—the professional painter, for example, has nothing but contempt for the amateur painter, the Sunday painter, the man who makes painting a spare-time recreation. On the other hand, there is a widespread contempt, among people who consider themselves cultured,

---

[7] *To Hell with Culture* (New York, 1964).

for the technologist, the specialist in scientific research or industrial production. That was the theme of Lord Snow's famous tract on the two cultures, the two irreconcilable factions within our society. That this social division should have come about, and should threaten the security of our civilization, is entirely the fault of a false system of education. The seeds of this division are sown at an early age, when it is ordained that a scientist need have no grammar, and a grammarian no science. So long as that dichotomy exists at the heart of our educational system, so long one of the primary tasks of adult education will be to heal the divided heart. In the end humanism is neither scientific nor academic: it is simply human. The task is not, as Sir Eric Ashby would have it, to confer values on the automatic factory: the automatic factory is inhuman, and we must never accept its inhumanity as a value to be reconciled with human values. Our task is rather to set aside the automatic factory as something that has nothing whatsoever to do with human values, and to turn once again to man in his dereliction. Man has been cast out of that cybernetic paradise: like Adam and Eve he must now cultivate a wilderness.

That great soul, the young French philosopher who died of starvation during the Second World War, Simone Weil, worked for a whole year in an automatic factory—by deliberate choice lived the life of a worker on the production line. What she found there was a universal degradation of the human spirit. The workers in an automatic factory, she says, are denied even the last resource of a slave—stoicism. The work they live by, with its unvarying succession of mechanical movements and rapid rhythm, allows them only the stimulus of fear and of the pay-check. To indulge in a sentiment like stoicism would put them off their stroke. It is simpler, and involves least suffering, to conform to the mechanical rhythm. What kind of adult education shall we offer such people? And, as I said earlier, they are the rank and file of our technological civilization. For such people technology has no values, has no standards of excellence and taste; for such people technology is slavery. For such people automation is salvation.

But what shall we do with these salvaged robots? We must give them some purpose in life, some function in society, for otherwise they will not know what to do with their new-found freedom. After her experience in the Renault factory Simone Weil wrote:

Education—whether its object be children or adults, individuals or an entire people, or even oneself—consists in creating motives. To show what is beneficial, what is obligatory, what is good—that is the task of education. Education concerns itself with the motives for effective action. For no action is ever carried out in the

absence of motives capable of supplying the indispensable amount of energy for its execution.[8]

This seems to me to be the essential truth about
education, but apart from the question of means
which Simone Weil proceeds to discuss, there is involved a choice of motives. Simone Weil was a mystic.
Physical labour, she said, is a daily death; and like
death itself a thing of necessity, not of choice:

> The world only gives itself to Man in the form of
> food and warmth if Man gives himself to the
> world in the form of labour.

Consent to this law, which makes work indispensable for conserving life, represents the most perfect act of obedience that is given to Man to
accomplish, and therefore, concludes Simone Weil,
physical labour should be the spiritual core in a well-
ordered social life. But this is hardly a motive that
would give new impetus to adult education, and it is
a little difficult to see how such a spiritual attitude
differs from the stoicism which elsewhere Simone
Weil has found incompatible with work in an automatic factory. Our task is neither to reconcile the
worker to a daily death nor to provide the consola-
tions of literature and art from a cultural past com-

---

[8] *The Need for Roots,* trans. Arthur Wills (London, 1952), pp.
181–2.

pletely outside the experience of a technological age. Our task—our limited task—is to introduce values and motives into the daily life and activities of ordinary people, values and motives that will serve as a necessary stimulus to their spiritual development.

The motives and values I wish to introduce into adult education have a direct bearing on vocational activities. These values and motives are not adequately described as "standards of taste." Taste is a middle-class virtue, a retrospective eclecticism that has little or nothing to do with the "visual thinking" that is lacking in our technological age. Our aim is to stimulate this visual thought, this sensuous apprehension of form in all its daily manifestations. The most neglected factor in education is the autonomous mental activity that is constantly at work transforming the multiplicity of visual impressions into apprehensible unities, forms that intuitively reflect our feelings. Every such act of visual cognition is itself an elementary artistic form, and education should be the natural cultivation of these elementary forms of visual cognition, their realization in expressive symbols that communicate vital feeling. Art is a principle of vital growth, an unfolding of inherent abilities to order perceptual experience, to cope with this experience cognitively by giving it unity of form. If we can concentrate on these inherent mental powers, cultivate them as we cultivate our powers of conceptual reasoning, then taste is no problem. It could conceivably be fed into the computer and determine the form of its products.

The practical problem remains, and I do not pretend to have given any clue to its solution. Each society, each community, must find its own solution, a solution compatible with its historical situation. Whatever we teach must be taught from a central core of interest, from a personal awareness of motive. I would not teach history to electronic engineers, or cosmology to aircraft designers. I would try to create motives in men and women that would fill their lives with creative energy. This creative energy, as I have tried to show, is latent in the human frame, and it is the measure of our failure that by no existing means of education can we release it. Indeed, we have to confess that we have unwittingly suppressed it, until the shaping spirit of imagination has passed from our conscious, academic culture, and only creeps back unrecognized in the workshops of a few new industries, such as the aircraft industry, industries without history and without cultural traditions, where the formative vision is free to follow harmonious principles of creation.

I think we have learned, in the earlier stages of education, that it is a vital mistake to separate education from play. In the same way, at the adult stage, I think it is a vital mistake to separate education from work. I could not conceive such a separation in my own case, but then I am an intellectual: my work is my education. But if this can be true of things created with words, or colours, or sounds, can it not also be true of everything that man creates, not only with his hands, but with machines? The real evil of the factory system, as has often been said, is that the worker has no interest in the form and function of the component he is producing. Automation may relieve him of some of the tedium of repetitive tasks, but he will be bored with life itself unless he can discover some creative purpose in all his work. We must, however, give a new meaning to the word work, and perhaps we shall discover that it does not then differ from play. We may remember Schiller's words, which I have often quoted, that man only plays when he is a man in the fullest meaning of the word, and is only completely man when he is playing. It would be one more ironic turn to man's history if the automation he so much fears were to provide him with the kind of freedom which he has so long sought. But that freedom will remain an illusion unless it is filled with the motives and the disciplines of a creative imagination.

VI

THE THIRD REALM OF EDUCATION

O<small>N THE LINTEL OF THE DOOR</small> to a stone house he built for himself in a moorland village in my native county of York, an ancestor of mine carved these words:

> By hammer and hand
> All arts do stand.

I cannot claim that this motto is the foundation of my philosophy of education, for it was comparatively late in my life that I discovered it. But it will serve as a text for this chapter, which is to be concerned with some aspects of the subject now neglected. I refer to the purpose of those creative and constructive activities which do indeed find a place at some stage in most educational systems under such headings as "crafts" or "projects," but are kept subordinate to the acquisition of knowledge. "At some stage" usually implies the primary stage: as the child's educational

career progresses, these activities give way to the
overwhelming demands of the curriculum, in which
"projects" become "subjects," and the memory is
trained to meet certain standards of knowledge determined by factors of an economic or even a political nature. Sometimes conscious efforts are made
to correct this bias, but they have about as much effect as a loose rein on a runaway horse. There is little prospect of altering the course of our educational
policy unless we can effect a revision of its fundamental concepts. Such a revision will require a close
look at some of the basic tendencies of our civilization.

There are as many definitions of the purpose of
education as there are philosophers of education, but
unless they have some sinister intention inspired by
political or theological motives, they all agree that
there is no education unless there is a discovery and
growth of faculties that otherwise remain indolent.
Coleridge's definition is as good as any I know: "Education of the Intellect by awakening the Method of
self-development." Such a method, Coleridge explained, does not reach after:

> . . . any specific information that can be con-
> veyed into it from without . . . [The aim is]
> not storing the passive Mind with the various
> sorts of knowledge most in request, as if the
> Human Soul were a mere repository or banquet-

ing room, but to place it in such relations of cir-
cumstance as should gradually excite its vegetat-
ing and germinating powers to produce new
fruits of Thought, new Conceptions, and Imagina-
tions, and Ideas.[1]

Coleridge, who always chose his words with care
for their meaning, suggests here that the method
of self-development, the only method capable of generating original thought, is the interaction of the
human soul and its physical environment, and in other
statements scattered throughout his works he makes it
clear that this method, which he did not hesitate to
call *scientific,* was dictated by nature herself.

. . . the simple truth, that as the forms in all
organized existence, so must all true and living
knowledge proceed from within; that it may
be trained, supported, fed, excited, but can never
be imposed or impressed.

It was far from my original intention to take Coleridge as my mentor on this occasion—his own career
illustrates a gradual loss of sensibility due to excessive
intellection. But the substance of a true science of
education—"that most weighty and concerning of
all sciences," as he called it, is found in his works,

---

[1] "On Method," quoted from *Enquiring Spirit*, Kathleen Coburn,
ed., London, 1951. Cf. *The Friend*, III, pp. 176–8.

particularly in those essays collected under the title
of *The Friend;*[2] and I make my first appeal to Coleridge, rather than to Rousseau or Marx or some modern exponent of a true dialectic of education, because he recognized this truth even when it told
against his own achievements. The substance of Coleridge's philosophy of education is a quite conscious
dialecticism—he himself uses the word on occasion—
which bids us "find tongues in trees; books in the
running streams; sermons in stones; and good [that
is, some useful end answering to some good purpose]
in every thing." He asserts:

> In a self-conscious and thence reflecting being,
> no instinct can exist without engendering the be-
> lief of an object corresponding to it, either pres-
> ent or future, real or capable of being realized;
> much less the instinct, in which humanity itself
> is grounded;—that by which, in every act of
> conscious perception, we at once identify our
> being with that of the world without us, and yet
> place ourselves in contra-distinction to that
> world.[3]

Coleridge apologized for the want, in his essays,
of illustrative examples, "occasioned by the haunting
dread of being tedious." I am possessed by the same

---

[2] References are to Henry Nelson Coleridge's ed. in 3 vols. (4th
ed.; London, 1850).

[3] *Ibid.*, p. 170.

haunting dread, but I shall proceed to develop this philosophy of education, perhaps in a direction which Coleridge himself would not have authorized, but mindful of his requirement, that before we can learn to recognize man in nature, we must first learn to comprehend nature in man, and its laws in the ground of existence.[4] In other words, our approach to the problem must be primarily psychological.

There is a sense in which, as human beings, we must prefer the organic to the inorganic, the process of growth to the stability of achievement, life to death: between birth and dissolution we are sustained by a vital or erotic impulse. But there is also a sense in which, as members of an organized community, we must prefer law to self-will, discipline to disorder, the ego to the id. Education is a mediation between such extremes, but it must be conceived as a dialectical process. All vital growth tends towards and achieves harmonious form by means of such a dialectic. Transformation might be the name for such a dialectical process when society is the organism and civilization the aim. But as technology advances we are compelled to admit, whether we belong to capitalist or to communist societies, that instead of transformation into a harmonious society, we tend inevitably towards a social disharmony or schizophrenia to which the name *alienation* has been given.

---

[4] Cf. *ibid.*, p. 190.

Alienation, or self-estrangement (the German word used by Marx is *Entfremdung*) is a direct consequence of the divison of labour, and according to Marx begins to make its appearance in the history of society as soon as there is a separation between self-activity and activity for the common interest. As long as a cleavage exists between the particular and the common interest, Marx argues, man's own deed becomes an alien power opposed to him, which enslaves him instead of being controlled by him. When labour is measured and distributed, each man has a task assigned to him, from which he cannot escape. A contradiction is established between the interest of the individual and that of the community, and to maintain the common interest that social power which we call the State comes into being. As the division of labour becomes more and more remote from the individual's immediate needs, so this social power takes on the character of an alien force, existing outside the individual, of the origin and end of which he is ignorant, whose functioning he can by no means control. "The division of labour," Marx wrote,

> implies from the outset the division of the *conditions of labour,* of tools and materials, and thus the splitting up of accumulated capital among different owners, and thus, also, the division between capital and labour, and the different

forms of property itself. The more the division of labour develops and accumulation grows, the sharper are the forms which this power of differentiation assumes. Labour itself can only exist on the premise of this fragmentation.[5]

Ruskin expressed the same idea more vividly in *The Stones of Venice.*

We have much studied and much perfected, of late, the great civilized invention of the division of labour; only we give it a false name. It is not, truly speaking, the labour that is divided; but the men:—Divided into mere segments of men—broken into small fragments and crumbs of life; so that all the little piece of intelligence that is left in a man is not enough to make a pin, or a nail, but exhausts itself in making the point of a pin or the head of a nail.[6]

---

[5] *The German Ideology,* Karl Marx and Friedrich Engels, ed. R. Pascal; trans. Lough and Magill, Parts I and II (London, 1938), p. 65.

[6] *The Stones of Venice,* II, vi, s. 16. Ruskin already perceived that the division of labour implies "a perpetual and exquisitely timed palsy." That the measurement of time is of the essence of the process is also the conclusion of the present-day sociologist. Cf. Daniel Bell, "Meaning in Work: a New Direction": ". . . the root of alienation lies *not* in the machine . . . but in the concept of efficiency. . . . Central to the idea of efficiency is a notion of measurement. Modern industry, in fact, began not with the factory —the factory has been known in ancient times—but with measurement. Through measurement we passed from the division of labour into the division of time." *Dissent,* VI, No. 3 (1959), pp. 246–7.

Alienation might therefore be defined as a division of the productive forces of society that leaves on the one side immensely complex structures, dehumanized and now almost completely automatic, and on the other side individuals with no self-determined activity, linked to these complex structures by non-productive energies which we still call labour.

I shall leave out of account the political implications of this situation, which were Marx's main concern, and would concentrate on the mental or psychological consequences of such an estrangement. Not that Marx was neglectful of these other consequences. Indeed, one may say that the whole Marxian theory of knowledge depends on the maintenance of a total involvement of man's sensible faculties with his material environment. On a constant interaction of Man and Nature depends the whole dialectical theory of existence—the conception of man:

> . . . confronting nature as one of her own forces, setting in motion arms and legs, heads and hands, the natural forces of his body, in order to appropriate nature's productions in a form suitable to his own wants.

This is Marx's own formulation in *Capital*,[7] and he continues:

---

[7] *Capital: a Critical Analysis of Capitalist Production*, ed. Friedrich Engels; trans. Moore and Aveling (London, 1886), pp. 156–7.

> By thus acting on the external world and chang-
> ing it, he [man] at the same time changes his
> own nature. He develops the potentialities that
> slumber within him and subjects these inner
> forces to his own control.

Marx then makes an important distinction that has
been greatly intensified by the development of technology since Marx's time.

The human and instinctive form of labour is exercised directly by the physical energies of the body
and is directed towards what Marx calls Nature. Marx
made a very close analysis of the elementary factors
of the labour process, distinguishing between the personal activity of man, work itself, the subject of that
work, and its instruments. He showed that when resolved into its elementary factors work is human
action with a view to the production of "use-values,"
that is to say, the appropriation of natural substances
to human requirements. Such work is "the necessary
condition for effecting exchange of matter between
man and Nature; it is the everlasting Nature-imposed
condition of human existence, and therefore is independent of every social phase of that existence, or
rather, is common to every such phase."[8] He then goes
on to make his fundamental distinction between labour
for the production of use-value, common to all phases
of human existence, and labour for the production of

---

[8] *Ibid.*, pp. 163–4.

surplus-value, characteristic of the capitalist system. Immensely important as this distinction is for his critical analysis of capitalist production, as Marx develops the distinction we tend to lose sight of the concomitant difference in the quality of the labour processes involved—in fact, Marx relegates this distinction to a footnote, merely noting that:

> The English language has two different expressions for these two different aspects of labour; in the Simple Labour-process, the process of producing Use-Values, it is *Work;* in the process of creation of Value, it is *Labour,* taking the term in its strictly economical sense.[9]

This is substantially the distinction that has been elaborated by subsequent writers, notably by Hannah Arendt and Herbert Marcuse.[10]

---

[9] *Ibid.,* p. 166.

[10] Cf. Hannah Arendt, *The Human Condition* (Chicago: University of Chicago Press, 1958); Herbert Marcuse, *Eros and Civilization* (London and New York, 1956).

Mrs. Arendt points out that "every human language, ancient and modern, contains two etymologically unrelated words for what we have come to think of as the same activity, and retains them in the face of their persistent synonymous usage." Her remarkable book *The Human Condition* is a profound exploration of the social significance of this distinction, but it should be noted that Marx's use of the two words becomes reversed, for Mrs. Arendt follows Locke, who distinguishes between the labour of our body and the work of our hands—*animal laborans* and *homo*

We may next note that in the creation of surplus-value, capitalist production developed not only technological processes designed to increase production, but also an increasingly refined division of labour designed to make these technological processes more and more efficient and therefore more profitable. The technological revolution further intensified the distinction between work and labour. Not only was the worker alienated to an even greater degree from any direct contact with his raw materials, that is to

---

faber. It was Adam Smith and Karl Marx, as she points out, who were responsible for converting this fundamental distinction into a distinction between productive and unproductive labour, modified by subsequent economists into the distinction between skilled and unskilled labour. Marx's originality lies in his perception that a man's labour, especially by modern methods of production, would suffice for more than his individual needs; and that the whole economy of capitalism was to be explained; and attacked, on the inability of the system to distribute such surplus values justly.

Mrs. Arendt distinguishes a third human activity, which she calls *action,* by which she means not only the human condition of plurality, the necessity of coming to terms with our fellow men, but the whole process of living, of coming to terms with our existential situation. This kind of human activity is not our present concern: we speak of the *work* of art, and Mrs. Arendt quite rightly discusses art as a product of *homo faber,* as the reification and materialization of thought. I quarrel a little with her description of works of art as "thought things," for I believe that in a certain fundamental sense art is cognitive, a mode of apprehending the unknown and making it real; but in so far as she insists that "works of art are the most intensely worldly of all tangible things," and are "the work of our hands," she is clarifying the educative nature of this particular kind of work.

say, from the objects of labour spontaneously provided by Nature, but he found himself separated from the satisfaction that is normally derived from the realization of a specific product in its wholeness.

Modern technological production includes a vast range of processes and I am not suggesting that they all exclude the element of personal control: that none of them engages sensuous human activity. Primitive technology may still be regarded "as a mere extension of bodily skills employed for the satisfaction of bodily appetites." This is an observation of Professor Michael Polanyi, who continues:

> And even in highly complex and predominantly articulate branches of technology, like the manufacture of cloth and the production of steel, there is involved a measure of unspecifiable know-how which is essential to the efficiency of labour and the quality of its product.

But in general, as Polanyi then points out, "technology teaches only actions to be undertaken for *material* advantages by the use of *implements* according to (more or less) *specifiable rules*,"[11] a definition which I find conclusive, especially when further clarified by the footnote attached to it, which points out that "material advantages" would exclude *inter alia* the achievement of symbolic expression or of human in-

---

[11] *Personal Knowledge* (London, 1958), pp. 175–6.

teractions, and that action according to "specifiable rules" would exclude artistic performances.

The Marxian dialectic is based on the assumption that labour is a process "in which man of his own accord starts, regulates, and controls the material reactions between himself and Nature." The whole Marxian theory demands that knowledge should be based on a direct perception of reality, of sense data, separate impressions received through the senses and defined, connected, classified and finally verified in practice. Further, this sensuous human activity, which gives man a reasoned relation to the surrounding world, increases with the development of the instruments of production, with the perfecting of technical devices, so long as these are extensions of the senses.

> The microscope, the telescope, the most accurate measuring instruments, etc., assist in the enrichment of sensed material, in the human perception of the surrounding world, and by this means create a basis for ever wider and deeper generalizations.[12]

Marxist philosophy admits, therefore, not only that theory and practice interact with one another in dialectical progression, but that the development of

---

12 M. Shirokov, *A Textbook of Marxist Philosophy*, trans. A. C. Moseley (London, n.d.), p. 110.

our understanding depends on the continuous engagement of our senses, which develop and are perfected along with the development of the instruments of production. What Marxist philosophy could not anticipate and does not recognize is that productive processes have now reached a stage of automation in which the senses are no longer in contact with the objective world, that no refinement of hearing or taste, no training of the eye, is now involved in the concrete practice of technological man. In other words, the distinction that now prevails between what Polanyi calls "the operational principles of technology" and the heuristic principles of science is one that destroys the foundations of dialectical materialism. Deprived of any practice in the sensuous meaning of the word, man can only elaborate a new kind of idealism as divorced from the reality as the idealism that Marx attacked. Meanwhile, with supreme disregard for the consequences, the triumphant followers of Marx devote all their energies to the development of technological processes whose only purpose is utilitarian—i.e., the production of more and more consumer goods, regardless of the fact that such processes deepen and prolong that alienation of man foreseen by Marx more than a hundred years ago.

We may now see how all things conspire to complete the alienation of man. In the first stage of the history of capitalist production the worker is deprived of a direct relationship with or personal responsibility for the objects he produces. In the second stage the operational principles of technology—division of labour, mass production, automation—deprive labour of every sensuous relationship to natural materials. Work itself is "processed," de-sensualized, de-materialized, with profound effects on the whole balance of civilization.

The purpose of all this directed labour and mass production is, of course, to produce an age of abundance and leisure, and as we get nearer to that age we begin to realize that we are threatened by appalling moral and social problems. Society suffers from a disorientation of its profoundest instincts, with psychological consequences which are only just beginning to reveal themselves. Those instincts—basically the erotic instincts—have hitherto been diverted—or sublimated, as the psychoanalysts say—and transformed into constructive energies, visibly embodied in our civilization. The character of the energies now engaged by technological modes of production is so radically different from the character of the energies engaged by *work*, whether primitive or skilled, that the sublimating process itself must be affected.

Freud's hypothesis, which until recently was never seriously questioned, was that work provides a "very considerable discharge of libidinal component impulses, narcissistic, aggressive and even erotic."[13] This

13 *Civilization and Its Discontents* (London, 1949), p. 34.

formula has recently been challenged by two American psychologists, Herbert Marcuse and Norman Brown, precisely on the grounds that I am now challenging it in relation to the policy of the integration of theory and practice in education: namely, that it makes no distinction between alienated and non-alienated labour, between toil and work. The problem may be stated thus: If the alienated labour characteristic of modern technological processes of production no longer effects that sublimation of erotic instincts upon which our civilization, in its economic and moral aspects, is built, and assuming that these technological processes cannot now be reversed, then what substitute can we find which will fulfil the functions of unalienated or productive labour, that is to say, of work?

On a visit to the People's Republic of China in 1959, I was much struck by a prevailing awareness of the dialectical nature of the educational problem. To what extent the educational theories now being put into practice in that country are based on tradition was not altogether clear to me; tradition has been renewed and no doubt in the process account has been taken to some extent of the educational theories of the Western world. The main features of the Chinese system are determined, however, by a certain social philosophy which is perhaps a fusion of the dialectical materialism of Marx and Lenin with the dialectical universalism of Neo-Confucianism. It is possible to maintain, as does Dr. Joseph Needham, that the dialectical method of Marx originated in China—that Marx learnt it from Hegel, who learnt it from Leibniz, who derived it from the Jesuit missionaries in China with whom he corresponded. In any case, one does not have to go any further than the *Ta Hsüeh (Great Learning)* and the *Chung Yung (Doctrine of the Mean)*, two of the four Confucian classics, to find a "doctrine of the mean" which is in effect a dialectical philosophy of the most fundamental kind. When, therefore, the modern Chinese educator speaks of a policy of integration, as he always does, he is not conscious of any innovation. He is applying to a contemporary situation principles that have prevailed in China for twenty-five centuries. It is possible to argue, of course, that these principles are only too easily adapted to the collectivist ideology of the Communist Party in China; which demands, according to one writer:

. . . the implacable reduction of the individual to his social function rather than the promotion of his full individuality, uniqueness and originality, as in the West.[14]

But this implies a clash between educational and political ideals of which there is no evidence.

---

[14] Amaury de Riencourt, *The Soul of China* (London, 1959), p. 261.

Before describing how the Chinese apply these principles in their educational system, I ought perhaps to remind the reader how they were formulated in the Confucian classics I have mentioned, for they possess a striking actuality. The *Ta Hsüeh* explicitly declares in its first paragraph that one of the objects of education is "to renovate the people." Then, in a famous clause, it describes the educational process:

> The men of old who wished clearly to exemplify illustrious virtue throughout the world, first ordered well their own states. Wishing to order well their states, they first had to make an ordered harmony in their families. Wishing to do this, they first had to cultivate their individual selves. Wishing to do this, they first rectified their minds. Wishing to do this, they first had to seek for absolute sincerity in their thoughts. Wishing for absolute sincerity in their thoughts, they had first to extend their knowledge to the utmost. Such extension of knowledge lies in the investigation of things.

The next paragraph reverses the sequence of this chain of Great Learning, and thus we have an educational system which insists that the process of education begins with the investigation of things. All the early Confucians of the Ch'in and Han dynasties, and particularly the most realistic of them, the third century B.C. philosopher Hsün Tzu, had the same dialectical conception of both knowledge and learning. In one place Hsün Tzu states:

> Do you ask how to conduct the affairs of state? I would say: I have heard of cultivation of the person, but never of conducting affairs of state. The ruler is the form. When the form is correct, the shadow will be correct. The ruler is the basin. When the basin is round, the water in it will assume roundness. The ruler is the cup. When the cup is square, the water in it will assume squareness.[15]

The implication is, of course, that if the ruler of the state sets a good personal example, there will be no need for laws. But the precept is given a realistic, almost a materialistic application. Education is a process of conditioning, almost in the Pavlovian sense. "A five-inch foot-rule is the proper standard for the entire world"—that is how the *Ta Hsüeh* puts it. The perfection of the individual proceeds from a direct knowledge of his material environment, and the deeper his knowledge of his environment, the nearer he will approach to the *Tao* of nature, the universal harmony, the way of Heaven *(Ch'eng)*. Such being the essential doctrine of Confucianism, there was no

---

[15] Fung Yu-Lau, *A History of Chinese Philosophy,* trans. Derk Bodde, vol. I (Peiping and London, 1947), p. 365.

need to go to Marx or any of the Russian theorists
for a justification of an educational policy which at
every stage seeks an integration of theory and practice, of mental study and manual work.

In modern Chinese education this policy of integration is given a practical application which when
one first meets it seems almost naïve. I visited several
universities and colleges in different provinces of
China, and everywhere I found a doctrine of integration in force. All students are required to spend from
two to three months every year in productive labour,
in the factories or in the fields, and it is claimed that
such alternation of theory and practice has a vital-
izing effect on their mental development. It also leads
to a cross-fertilization of ideas between the sciences
and the arts, and to a humanistic outlook shared by
students of all subjects.

I found no evidence that this policy of integration
is in any way inspired by our Western psychology,
however much it may be justified by it. There is
in the Chinese Republic a general attitude in all social
problems which they call "the policy of walking on
two legs," and this general policy may refer to any
dialectical situation. It is used, for example, to refer
to the desirability of maintaining a healthy balance
between town and country, between industry and
agriculture, but in particular to indicate a healthy
balance between theory and practice in any subject,
and between the humanities and the sciences in edu-

cation as a whole. The practice may vary from university to university, from province to province, but I found that in Chin Hua University, the great technological institution near Peking, which in 1959 had about 12,000 students, 38 weeks were devoted to theory and research, 8 weeks to practical work in a factory, and 2 weeks to agricultural work, leaving 6 weeks for vacations. At the South-West Normal College near Chungking, a training college for teachers for middle or secondary schools, 34 weeks were given to theory and research, 10 to productive labour, and again 6 for vacations. It should be noted, however, that a certain proportion of the productive labour is carried out on the campus. A university may be equipped with its own forges and factories, capable of producing, in addition to laboratory equipment, quite complicated machine tools. Most colleges also have their own farms and market gardens to produce the food for the college canteens. But the educational program requires that the student spend a substantial period of his year off the campus, side by side with the peasants and factory workers. The social (as distinct from the educational) purpose of this requirement will be obvious.

Such a policy aims at an integration of theory and practice within each faculty. The integration of art and science, of technology and the humanities, over the whole educational system is also borne in mind, but is subject to the requirements of State planning.

There is the same drive to train technocrats as we find in the West, but some steps are taken to encourage a general level of culture. I noticed, when going round the library at Chin Hua University, some book-stacks of poetry, and when my surprise was evident, it was explained to me that all technological students were expected to make themselves familiar with the classical Chinese poets. Much time and encouragement are given to dramatic productions, fine art groups, poetry recitals and inter-departmental discussion groups.

In 1959 Chinese education had not been walking on two legs long enough for any general effects to be observable in the post-revolutionary culture of China—only ten years had elapsed since the formation of the Republic and the reorganization of the universities had been an immense task. I offer this Chinese evidence to show that where there is a will there is a way. The integration of theory and practice, of brainwork and handwork, is a possibility if the will to integration exists. Moreover, it has been proved that such integration has positive effects on the general level of intelligence. I have suggested that it exists in China because there is a tradition, which after two thousand years is an unquestioned assumption, namely, that education must begin with self-development, and that productive work is an essential phase of such education.

Before we can accept the Chinese system as an ideal

solution of our own educational problems, we must look a little closer into its cardinal assumptions. I shall examine these from a general and not specifically Chinese point of view. There seem to me to be three such cardinal assumptions, beginning with this basic assumption that self-development is the ideal method of education. "From the Son of Heaven down to the common people, all must consider cultivation of the person to be fundamental," as the *Ta Hsüeh* puts it.

This is not in itself an unusual assumption. From the ancient Greek sages to Plato and Aristotle, from the philosophers of the Enlightenment to Coleridge and our modern psychologists, what we now call the integration of the personality has been given as the chief aim of education, whether public or private. But throughout the history of our Western world, however eloquently this aim might be expressed by philosophers, however urgently it might be recommended by psychologists, it has remained an ideal, only attained by exceptional individuals, individuals so exceptional that we call them saints or mystics. Even in the Chain of Learning described in the *Ta Hsüeh*, some link always seems to break and thus prevent the common people, to use the Chinese expression, from becoming a community of superior men. The fault in the chain may be due to the weakness of the metal of which it is made; that is the explanation we call original sin. Or, as the Chinese tend to believe, it may be due to a lack of skill in the forging of the metal.

The doctrine of original, and on this earth irremediable, sin has one advantage: it excuses us from any further consideration of the problem as posed by the Confucians. If when the basin is round the water in it insists on being square, and when the cup is square the water stays round, then the form of the paradigm is immaterial. If knowledge of the nature of things can never be complete or thoughts never be sincere, then minds cannot be harmonized nor the personality integrated. Education, on such an assumption, can only be regimentation or regulation, and a self-attained and self-sustained equilibrium is therefore a false analogy drawn from the physical world and not applicable to the spiritual world. The Chinese philosophers recognize imperfection in man and perfection in Heaven: they differ from the Christian philosophers in assuming that this Heaven is a "way" that can be realized in life by means of instruction and discipline. Through self-enlightenment we can achieve absolute sincerity, that highest state of human development which is seen as a union of the inner and the outer. Such a state of absolute sincerity, which in Chinese is called *ch'eng,* is the way of Heaven, perfection of nature and perfection of the self, a single embracing state of bliss.

The doctrine of education through self-integration has parallels in Western psychology, if not in Western educational practice. I refer to what is known as the process of individuation in Jungian psychology, and psychoanalytical therapy as a whole is designed to effect a reconciliation between the individual and his social and familial environment. Though there have been attempts to extend this individualistic therapy to the group,[16] it cannot be said that any country in the West has made such integration the primary purpose of its educational system. But in China there is such a conscious determination.

The second cardinal assumption found in the Chinese educational policy is the assumption that theory and practice are unified in productive labour, and the labourer thereby becomes mentally and physically integrated. But everything in such an assumption will depend on the nature of the labour that is called "productive," for as Marx was always pointing out, the very consciousness of man depends on the material conditions determining production. If theory is to be unified with practice, it is very essential to ensure that the practice is human, that is to say, free from physical and moral constraint. That, at any rate, was the whole point of Marx's criticism of the alienation of man in capitalist production.

My contention is that the alienated labour of an advanced technological civilization can never provide

---

16 Notably by Trigant Burrow. See *The Biology of Human Conflict* (New York, 1937). Cf. pages 101–4.

that integration of theory and practice, of man and nature, demanded alike by the Chinese tradition of education and by our own realization of the social and psychological consequences of alienation. There exists no possibility, in modern technological processes of production, even in agriculture, of giving man that dialectical relationship to his material environment which will "develop the potentialities that slumber within him" and ensure the growth of his understanding. If work can no longer fulfil this function, to what alternative activity shall we turn?

The answer is to be found in the word which is the antithesis of *work*, namely *play*. We have been celebrating the two hundredth anniversary of the man who first provided this answer, Friedrich Schiller; but hitherto, perhaps because economic developments had not brought matters to a crisis, we have ignored his profound message. We can no longer afford to neglect Schiller's *Letters on Aesthetic Education*, which I have for many years regarded as the foundation of any realistic educational policy for our age of alienation. As Professor Norman Brown, whose name I have already mentioned, has said:

> History is transforming the question of reorganizing human society and human nature in the spirit of play from a speculative possibility to a realistic necessity. The most realistic observers are emphasizing man's increasing alienation from

his work; the possibility of mass unemployment
—i.e., liberation from work—given by modern
technology; and the utter incapacity of human
nature as it is today to make genuinely free use
of leisure—to play.[17]

And to reinforce his statement he quotes the diagnosis of one of the greatest and most realistic of
twentieth-century economists, John Maynard Keynes.

There is no country and no people who can
look forward to the age of leisure and abundance
without a dread.[18]

I do not wish for my part to consider the problem
solely in the terms of a future age of leisure and
abundance. The problem is equally urgent in a country like China, which is many decades away from such
an age; but China, in its wisdom, is anticipating the
problem and that is the reason why I continue to
mention its example—anticipating the problem, but
not, as I have indicated, finding the right solution.

I have said that Schiller has been neglected: it would
also be true to say that in general he has been misunderstood. Only Ernst Cassirer seems to have
grasped the essential difference between Schiller's

---

[17] *Life Against Death* (London, 1959), pp. 34–5.
[18] *Essays in Persuasion* (London and New York, 1932), pp.
366–7.

theory of play and the various biological and sociological theories of play represented by such names
as Darwin, Spencer, Huizinga and even Freud. As
Cassirer says:

> It is difficult to find a point of contact between
> the views of Schiller and modern biological
> theories of art. In their fundamental tendency
> these views are not only divergent but in a
> sense incompatible. The very term 'play' is
> understood and explained in Schiller's accounts
> in a sense quite different from that of all subse-
> quent theories. . . . Schiller's is a transcendental
> and idealistic theory; Darwin's and Spencer's
> theories are biological and naturalistic. For
> (Schiller) play is not a general organic activity
> but a specifically human one. . . . To speak of
> an analogy, let alone an identity, between human
> and animal play or, in the human sphere, be-
> tween the play of art and the so-called games of
> illusion, is quite alien to Schiller. To him
> this analogy would have appeared to be a basic
> misconception.[19]

This is the first point to establish: the unique character of human play, which is a world of freedom
and creativity, belonging to the intelligible and not
the phenomenal world, and therefore the antithesis
of work. But even Cassirer seems to have some dif-

---

[19] *Essays on Man* (New York, 1953), pp. 210–11.

ficulty in passing from this world of freedom and creativity to the world of art, which he describes as a world of contemplation or reflection; and he suggests that this conscious and reflective attitude marks the boundary between play and art. But such a boundary line does not really exist: as educators know, there is a gradual transition from the intuitively formative activities of the child to the still intuitively *trans*formative activities of the artist. The point is important and the whole case for the place of art in education rests on the continuity of a basic play activity, carried through from play to art and remaining distinct from those constructive and rational activities which are better included under the term work. Cassirer asserts:

> Artistic imagination always remains sharply distinguished from that kind of imagination which characterizes our play activity.

I doubt this assertion: I think it must have been based on a singularly limited experience of the range and variety of the child's imaginative activities. "The child plays with *things*, the artist plays with *forms*, with lines and designs, rhythms and melodies," Cassirer suggests, and to justify this distinction continues:

> In a playing child we admire the facility and quickness of transformation. The greatest tasks

are performed with the scantiest means. Any piece of wood may be turned into a living being. Nevertheless, this transformation signifies only a metamorphosis of objects into forms. In play we merely rearrange and redistribute the materials given in sense perception. Art is constructive and creative in a deeper sense. . . . A child does not live in the same world of rigid empirical facts as the adult. The child's world has a much greater mobility and transmutability. Yet the playing child, nevertheless, does no more than exchange the actual things of his environment for other possible things. No such exchange as this characterizes genuine artistic activity. . . . For the artist dissolves the hard stuff of things in the crucible of his imagination, and the result of this process is the discovery of a new world of poetic, musical, or plastic forms.[20]

Adequate as this is as a description of artistic activity, I think it merely describes a difference of degree and not of kind. I have given the evidence elsewhere,[21] and must content myself with a counter-assertion. There is, in all free artistic activity in children, an instinctive activity of a formative nature, only distinct from a fully developed artistic activity in that its power of concentration is directed to the intelligible rather than the phenomenal world. The child

[20] *Ibid.*, p. 209.
[21] See *Education Through Art* (2nd ed.; London, 1958).

gives intelligible form to its sensations and feelings rather than to its perceptions; but form it is; the imagination, as Schiller says, finally makes, in its attempt at a *free form,* the leap to aesthetic play! From this fact derive the cognitive and propaedeutic functions of art in education.

I have approached my main point by a long detour, but perhaps it is now in sight. Work in a technological civilization, work "undertaken for *material* advantages by the use of *implements* according to (more or less) *specifiable rules*" (to repeat Polanyi's comprehensive definition) no longer provides an education of the five senses, on which, as Marx realized, depends a development of our understanding of the objective world. Not only is a fundamental thesis of dialectical philosophy frustrated in technological production, in so much as practice no longer secures "the unity and mutual conditioning of the sensed and the logical moments of knowledge" (Shirokov's phrase); not only is "the cognitive function of sensuousness" minimized (Marcuse's phrase); but more seriously those repressed instincts upon which our civilization is built lack all constructive outlet. This negation inherent to our technological civilization must be resolved; and since it cannot now be resolved in work, it must be resolved in the development of the only impulse that is left undeveloped in our civilization, aesthetic play. The only development of the play impulse that is adequate for this task of reconciliation and reconstruction is its development into creative art. This was Schiller's great and prophetic conception. Schiller conceived "a total revolution in the mode of perception and feeling," a leap as decisive as Kierkegaard's leap into faith. In Schiller's description:

> A leap we must call it since a wholly new force now comes into play; for here, for the first time, the legislative faculty interferes with the operations of a blind instinct, subjects the arbitrary process of imagination to its immutable and eternal unity, imposes its own self-dependence upon the variable and its infiniteness upon the sensuous.[22]

In such words Schiller is linked, not only to Coleridge who came after him and was influenced by him, but also to Plato, and to those Confucian philosophers I have quoted. Schiller's eloquent conclusion, at once idealistic and realistic, will stand for all these mentors:

> In the midst of the awful realm of powers, and of the sacred realm of laws, the aesthetic creative impulse is building unawares a third joyous realm of play and of appearance, in which it releases mankind from all the shackles of circumstance and frees him from everything that may be called constraint, whether

[22] *On the Aesthetic Education of Man,* trans. Reginald Snell (London, 1954), p. 134.

physical or moral. . . . *To grant freedom by means of freedom* is the fundamental law of this kingdom.[23]

---

[23] *Ibid.*, p. 137.

VII

CULTURE AND EDUCATION
IN A WORLD ORDER

1. A CULTURAL CRISIS

WRITING TO NIETZSCHE in 1887, the Danish critic Georg Brandes rejected the title "an apostle of culture," which Nietzsche had wished to confer on him. "All apostolic mission-work has become to me an abomination," he said. Further:

> I am acquainted with only moralizing missionaries, and I am afraid that I am not altogether orthodox in my belief as to what is understood by culture. Is there anything at all inspiring in our culture taken as a whole, and who can conceive of an apostle without inspiration?

To this Nietzsche replied:

> You should not repudiate the expression "apostle of culture." In these days one cannot be more of

an apostle of culture than by making a mission
of his unbelief in culture.

I must begin by warning the reader that I set out
from this same point of view. Naturally I speak as
a European, and it is possible that my point of view
is not only limited, but even enveloped in a spectacular
twilight. In 1887 culture in Europe was an established
order, a monumental structure of prosperous cities
and peaceful universities, of respected scholars and
popular poets, of universal exhibitions and expanding
knowledge. Tasteless and stupid as it might be, ex-
asperating to geniuses like Nietzsche, Brandes and
Burckhardt, yet it did exist—solid, self-satisfied, and
apparently everlasting.

When we survey the intellectual life of Europe today, the contrast is overwhelming. Great cities have
been destroyed in two world wars and their scholars
scattered. The instruments of culture, libraries, printing presses, paper factories, were destroyed, and
though they have been reconstructed, a tradition has
been broken. Europe is still divided physically and
ideologically into two irreconcilable entities. In the past
such material difficulties have often constituted a challenge which, to adopt Toynbee's formula, has pro-
voked a cultural response. But nowhere in Europe
today can we find convincing evidence either of a
vital movement of ideas or of an affirmative attitude in the arts. Europe is materially bankrupt and

mentally exhausted. We cannot escape the conclusion that the epoch which began with the Renaissance, and which, in spite of interruptions and sudden checks, has formed a coherent tradition for more than five centuries, is now at an end. It is not a question of violent destruction, or of political disruption. These are the visible consequences of two world wars within a period of thirty years. Invisibly an inner disease, a canker, as we call it, has been eating away the sources of our European vitality, and any realistic diagnosis must recognize that the cure is not one which can be adequately defined by words like planning and reconstruction. A new source of vitality, springing up within the body itself, must be discovered and released. It is not now a question of making a mission of one's unbelief in culture: culture in that sense is dead or dying, and what we must now consider is the possible germination of a new culture.

The notion of a doomed civilization has been current for some time, and a form of historicism which gives to civilization an organic life-cycle has been characteristic of our age. The most pessimistic of these philosophers of history, Oswald Spengler, offers us no hope, no remission of our doom. Arnold Toynbee, the English philosopher of history already mentioned, is not so pessimistic—he admits that an upward tilt in the declining graph of civilization may be possible if we can become sufficiently conscious of our plight and take appropriate action to avoid the downward drift. A similar attitude is taken up by C. G. Jung, and his diagnosis is all the more valuable in that he indicates certain methods of cure. I might mention other analyses and prescriptions of equal profundity—those of Alfred Weber and Karl Jaspers, for example—but they all agree in this: The only hope of saving our civilization lies in the spiritual or psychological sphere: civilization, that is to say, is dependent on culture: unless as a people we find a new vision, we shall perish.

2. THE AIMS OF UNESCO

Into this world situation, universally recognized as desperate, there has stepped an official body called the United Nations Educational, Scientific and Cultural Organization—UNESCO, for short—one of the specialized agencies provided for in the Charter of the United Nations. Its first general conference was held in Paris in November, 1946, and its constitution was then ratified. It has established its secretariat in Paris and has now built up an organization of considerable size and of almost unlimited scope.

UNESCO has been created as an immediate consequence of the war, and it is obvious from its printed constitution that the prevention of future wars is regarded as its primary task. That constitution opens with these words:

The Governments of the States parties to this Constitution on behalf of their Peoples declare: that since wars begin in the minds of men, it is in the minds of men that the defenses of peace must be constructed;

and it goes on to assert that:

ignorance of each other's ways and lives has been a common cause, throughout the history of mankind, of that suspicion and distrust between the peoples of the world through which their differences have all too often broken into war.

The constitution of UNESCO then announces the measures it will take to promote the intellectual and moral solidarity of mankind. They include:

full and equal opportunities for education for all; the unrestricted pursuit of objective truth; the free exchange of ideas and knowledge; the development and increase in means of communication;

or, more specifically:

the free flow of ideas by word and image through all means of mass communication; the giving of a fresh impulse to popular education and the spread of culture; the suggesting of educational methods best suited to prepare children for the responsibilities of freedom; the maintenance, increase and diffusion of knowledge, by assuring the conservation and protection of the world's inheritance of books, works of art and monuments of history and science; international exchange of persons active in the fields of education, science and culture; exchange of publications, objects of artistic and scientific interest and other materials of information; international co-operation calculated to give the people of all countries access to the printed and published materials produced by any of them.

Before examining these purposes and functions in more detail, I would like to point out that they are based on two unconscious assumptions: that culture is a concrete material which can be disposed of, handed round, bartered like butter or steel; and secondly, that this material culture is already stored up in universities, libraries and museums, waiting, like corn in Egypt, to be distributed to the hungry masses. Whereas, in reality, culture is a spiritual growth, for the most part very lowly, like the grass in the fields, but growing here and there into tall fruitful trees, rooted nevertheless in the soil; and culture, being this indigenous and perishable organic life, can be uprooted and diffused only by artificial means and in a state of artificial preservation. To continue the metaphor, and give the substance of what I am going to maintain, it is only the seeds of culture that can be diffused with any pervasive or creative result.

Before going on to express my own credo, I will now venture to characterize the ideals which have presided at the creation of UNESCO[1] a little more precisely. UNESCO is a reincarnation of the Institute for Intellectual Co-operation and the International Bureau of Education, bodies which functioned before the war under the aegis of the League of Nations. The deliberations of these bodies were conducted on a plane of intellectual abstraction—they were international debating societies with absolutely no effect on the course of events. It is true that they carried out some useful technical research—on the cleaning of paintings or the architecture of museums, for example—but their deliberations did not reach the common man, and their effect on the cultural situation in Europe was *nil*.

It is too early yet to charge UNESCO with the same intellectual bias and seclusion; but the programs it has so far undertaken betray an academic character; its policy so far shows the same reliance on conferences and committees; and in general there is

---

[1] More recently UNESCO has shown a welcome tendency to support independent organizations with specific functions—for example, the body mentioned on an earlier page, The International Society for Education through Art, which was founded in 1954.

the same tendency to confuse culture with learning, and education with propaganda. One of the main campaigns of UNESCO is directed against illiteracy. Here we see the prejudice of the scientific humanist, and scientific humanism is undoubtedly the intellectual atmosphere in which UNESCO has been conceived and is now being directed. To the scientific humanist it is axiomatic that knowledge, in the sense of knowledge about the structure of the universe, about the facts of life, about history, geography and economics —that such knowledge constitutes the basis of human progress and that it should therefore be as widely diffused as possible. If every inhabitant of the globe could be taught to read and write, and if UNESCO could provide them with what are called "objective textbooks of history," then the problem of the solidarity of mankind would seem, to the scientific humanist, to be largely solved.

3. INTELLECTUAL v. MORAL EDUCATION

The fallacy which underlies this type of reasoning is a heritage of our cultural development since the Renaissance, and is due to the separation which then took place between intellectual and moral education. The ancient Greek philosophers, particularly Plato and Aristotle, had always insisted that the minds and the emotions of children should be trained *pari passu,* in equal measure, step by step; and that if there was any question of priority, then the education of the emotions, moral or ethical education, should come first. The ideal put forward by UNESCO—"the unrestricted pursuit of objective truth"—would have been regarded by them as an extremely dangerous ideal. Objective truth, they would have said, must never be separated from subjective truth. Indeed, its scope should never exceed the limits set by subjective truth. The limits set by subjective truth are moral limits—limits, that is to say, determined by our sense of the good life, by our sense of a measure or harmony in the emotional and practical aspects of living.

What has happened since the Middle Ages is a gradual separation of these educational spheres. Owing to the identification of morality and religion—an identification which is an historical development, and has nothing to do with the essential nature of these two categories—the Christian church established its claim to control the moral education of children. This was satisfactory so long as the church also controlled the intellectual education of children. Within the Christian *Weltanschauung,* a development of the whole man was possible. But in the course of time, with the growth of scientific humanism and secularism, the church relinquished its control over intellectual education, retaining only the sphere of moral education.

The situation was bad enough when these two

systems of education proceeded efficiently but independently—in the seventeenth and eighteenth centuries, for example. You then had two opposed but equally strong forces competing for the control of society—a Bossuet or a Fénelon gradually yielding to Voltaire, Rousseau and the Encyclopaedists. During the nineteenth century, and at an increasing pace during our own century, the Christian church lost its authority within the States of Europe, and as a consequence it relinquished its essential function in society, the moral education of children. For all practical purposes moral education, in all but a few isolated communities, has entirely disappeared from our modern civilization.

The natural assumption is that, in order to restore moral education, we must re-establish the educational authority of the churches. But that is to forget that there is no essential connection between moral education as defined by pagan philosophers like Plato and Aristotle, and religious belief as required by the Christian church. In other words, it is logically conceivable, and in my opinion practically possible, to re-establish moral education without waiting for a religious revival. Indeed, I would go so far as to say that a religious revival, if that is our desire, is not conceivable until there has been a moral re-education of mankind. Ecstatic conversions, blind emotional drives such as we associate with names like Billy Graham or Aimee Semple MacPherson, do not lead to the establishment of true religion, which always requires, according to its profoundest theologians, the grounding of faith in reason; nor do religious revivals of a sectarian character necessarily promote social unity.

But it is morality itself, as a concept, which must first be revised. It has become hopelessly entangled with religious emotion, on the one hand, and, on the other hand, with a purely rationalistic or legalistic codification of right and wrong. But morality is neither a mystery nor a judgment. It is the exercise of a free choice. It is a spontaneous act of volition, and the only problem, as Plato realized, and as later educationalists like Pestalozzi and Herbart realized, is how to ensure that the will always jumps instinctively, so to speak, in the right direction.

It may be objected that I am not using the word morality in its accepted sense, and I must admit I would be happier with some other word if it existed. It is an ironic fact that in English-speaking countries when we wish to describe that social integrity which I conceive to be the proper meaning of morality, we use the word in its French form—we speak of the *morale* of a people. But a people with *morale*— that is to say, with a unity arising spontaneously out of its social activities with mutual aid as its inspiring purpose—such a people possesses in the surest sense the elements of morality, and these elements are all the stronger for not being consciously formulated.

The basis of morality is not in faith or in reason, but in a particular kind of discipline. Discipline is no mystery: it is a mechanism. The scientists call it a conditioned reflex. But everything, of course, depends on what our reflexes are conditioned to. Pavlov conditioned his dogs to respond to the ringing of a bell. By various experiments of that kind he could produce in animals, not merely a measurable flow of saliva, but complex emotional states corresponding to psychopathic symptoms in human beings. Human children can be conditioned even more easily than dogs, and because of their wide range of sensibility and intelligence, with infinitely subtler results. Modern psychologists, not to mention modern propagandists, recognize the perfect feasibility of conditioning the human mind, especially the still plastic mind of the child, to predetermined patterns of thought and behaviour.

The crucial question is the choice of the patterns. They can be arbitrary and ideological—the patterns imposed by the Jesuit, the Communist or the Nazi; but they can also be physical, when, if they are good patterns, we call them beautiful. The prototypes for such physical patterns are found in the objective world, in nature, in the formal structure of organic and inorganic phenomena. It was to the imitation of these prototypes that Plato first directed our attention. To come straight to the point, these prototypes are the patterns of virtue, to which all children should be conditioned. The whole burden of Plato's theory of education is to the effect that if only we bring up children in the contemplation of universal forms, in the practice of graceful and harmonious movements, in the active making of beautiful objects, then these children will instinctively recognize and choose goodness when they see it. Aesthetic education develops ethical virtue.

It is not my purpose, in this book, to give a detailed exposition of this theory of moral education. I am repeating certain ideas which are very clearly expressed by Plato. I can only beg the reader to return to the study of Plato if he feels any doubt, either about the priority of moral education or about the causal relationship which exists between moral virtue and aesthetic training. I have tried in a former book[2] to give these principles of aesthetic education a modern formulation; my purpose on this occasion is to bring into clear opposition two ideals and two implied policies—on the one hand, that which UNESCO announces as "the unrestricted pursuit of objective truth," and, on the other hand, that which I will call "the primacy of moral discipline."

At this point it might be objected that UNESCO does recognize the need for a moral policy, in declaring that "the defenses of peace must be constructed . . . in the minds of men," and again in speaking of

---

[2] *Education Through Art* (London, 1943), rev. ed., 1958.

the need to establish the "democratic principles of the dignity, equality and mutual respect of men," principles which are surely of a moral nature. But UNESCO, it will then be said, cannot intervene in matters which are so full of prejudice and irrationality as the moral discipline of nations. "The unrestricted pursuit of objective truth" is one thing—that is the famous objectivity of science, a logical positivism to which all nations, races and creeds must, if committed to the ideals of scientific humanism, give their assent. But a moral integrity of universal scope—a social unanimity in which white men and black men, Chinese and Eskimos, capitalists and communists, Christians and Buddhists, rationalists and mystics freely participate—that is not a project within the scope of UNESCO!

But nevertheless it is the only project that can secure the aims set forth by such an organization. If "wars begin in the minds of men," they are not to be prevented by card-indexes and encyclopaedias, by documentary films and the circulation of books on the subject. The minds of men are controlled only by some form of moral discipline. The question, therefore, is whether UNESCO, or any similar organization, can discover an effective method of securing the instinctive observance of certain moral disciplines. It is, to use our slang expression, "a tall order," but it has been attempted before. I have already referred to the methods of education proposed by Plato and

Aristotle, which they would have considered of universal application. I might now refer to those moral disciplines which have been the practical aspect of religions with a universal claim, such as Buddhism, Christianity and Mohammedanism. It is, of course, before the still powerful and conflicting claims of such religions that UNESCO hesitates to assert its authority. Even if eventually it has behind it the sanction of the United Nations and the atomic bomb itself, it will hardly venture to assert its authority against arbitrary interpretation of the voice of God. The unrestricted pursuit of objective truth at this point comes into conflict with that other aim announced by UNESCO—universal respect for the human rights and fundamental freedoms of the peoples of the world, without distinction of race, sex, language or religion.

We might, of course, attempt to discover a common ground of morality in the eleven religious systems which prevail in the world today, but the result would be an unpersuasive abstract of dogmas. And it would ignore the truth demonstrated by every great educator, that men are not governed by moral precepts: they are made moral by habitual practices. It may be that some realization of the moral dilemma which would face an organization committed to the principle of scientific humanism influenced the Communist members of the United Nations in their decision not to participate in UNESCO—the U.S.S.R.

and Yugoslavia have withheld their support from the organization. These nations have a very positive *Weltanschauung* of their own: they believe in a materialistic interpretation of history, and they cannot subscribe, therefore, to the very first principle announced in the constitution of UNESCO—that wars have their origins in the minds of men. According to the doctrinaire Marxist, wars have their origins in the economics of capitalist imperialism—in a sphere, that is to say, far more concrete than any covered by the phrase "the minds of men." I do not myself subscribe to this Marxist doctrine: it seems to me to be a simplification just as misleading as the intellectual explanation offered by the framers of UNESCO's constitution. Modern wars have their origins in the collective unconscious of mankind if in any specific region; they are symptoms of the moral nihilism which has released the latent predatory instincts of mankind, and they can only be prevented by a revolution in the social basis of human consciousness.

4. THE NECESSARY REVOLUTION

This moral revolution cannot be secured by intellectual propaganda addressed to minds already corrupted beyond redemption. A moral revolution is a total reorientation of the human personality, and can

be secured only by two methods, which might be
called (1) integration, and (2) education.

But *education*, it will be said, is the primary object of UNESCO: it has first place in its title and
strongest emphasis in its objectives. But what I mean
by education and what UNESCO means by education
are two entirely different things—the difference, in
short, between *moral* and *intellectual* education.

Further, the methods of moral education which I
propose are not the methods usually advocated by
ethical and religious organizations. Like these organizations, I recognize certain moral values—justice,
charity, freedom—but I do not believe that these
values can be realized or preserved by the methods
adopted by the churches. You can formulate moral
precepts, tables of law, commandments, and these
can be enforced by threats of punishment and eternal
damnation. In this way instincts that are socially inconvenient are driven underground where they fester
until they become destructive forces, erupting like
volcanoes with disastrous effects on the individual
and on society. Nothing has been so clearly demonstrated by modern psychology as the reciprocal relationship between frustration and aggression, both
in the individual and in society.

What is necessary, for our personal and social
health, is some method of guiding the destructive
energies of man into positive, creative channels, so
that no feelings of frustration ensue. That method is

known to some psychologists as "sublimation," to others as "the integration of the personality," and such sublimation or integration should be a normal phase of education—a natural process which every person undergoes without strain or compulsion. When, as in the case of the vast majority of adults in our diseased societies, that natural process of integration has never been achieved—has never, indeed, been attempted—then some form of analysis and some method of therapy become necessary. We have to call in the physician.

Let us ignore for the moment the desperate position of those who are already afflicted with psychic disorders, and ask what form education should take if we would avoid those disorders in the future.

When Plato and Aristotle insist on the priority of moral education, these philosophers are assuming that knowledge and power, all the attributes of science and learning, are not merely ineffective, but positively dangerous, unless they are used to promote the well-being of mankind. It is surely not necessary to demonstrate that axiom to a world cowering under the threat of the atom bomb! But in our present state of moral indecision, or moral *atrophy* as it should be called, no universal (i.e., politically effective) recognition is given to any moral values; or such recognition as is given is of a purely intellectual character, and has no emotional sanction. We recognize evil when it is objective—that is to say, when its social consequences are evident to our senses; but there is no compulsion to pursue good; good deeds are private deeds and are supposed to be their own rewards. We might say that our civilization has no natural habits of goodness—only certain intellectual concepts of goodness, some of which we try to enforce by legal sanctions.

Admittedly there are many decent people in the world today who aspire to the good life and conduct themselves in a manner which they would regard as sober, industrious and reasonable. But such people —our bourgeois selves—are secret promoters of our nihilistic decadence. We shrink from the violent extremes of fascism and totalitarianism, but that does not exempt us from seeking a solution of the problems which brought fascism and totalitarianism into being. In the state of our civilization today, moral passivity, even in the disguised shape of intellectual indifference, is no state of virtue. There were millions of good respectable citizens in Germany, and we can now see clearly that their inactivity was perhaps the greatest crime of all—certainly the decisive factor in a fateful situation.

It was not sufficient to stand aside in Pharisaic superiority. We are all implicated in the decadence of our civilization, and it is only to the extent that our dull indifference is fused to a white heat of moral indignation, and consequent moral activity, that the future can have any promise of greatness.

Positive virtue is active virtue, and active virtue reveals itself in a certain way of life, a natural happiness or playfulness which has almost disappeared from the world today. We may find the pattern of such a civilization in some remote corner of the globe—perhaps in the island of Bali, in some Mexican village, or in an Eskimo's igloo—not in the so-called civilized world, not in Europe. We might do worse than go to the Balinese or the Eskimos for a lesson in the art of living, for there we should find preserved the two essential secrets of moral education—intimacy and activity. For we cannot expect to create a moral consciousness by means of "mass media"—the radio, the press and the cinema. Nor can we create a moral influence by words if we confine words to their intellectual usage. The essential means are, as Plato argued, aesthetic activities: the sense of goodness and nobility is inculcated, ingrained in the living substance of the human being, by the practice of concrete arts, which alone have that basis of harmony and rhythm found in nature. Such harmonious forms and relationships are qualities or essences which we can disengage from the material universe. Some of their dimensions or operations may be available only to intuition or special forms of consciousness (the sense of absolute pitch in music, for example); others can be measured and recorded by the scientist—the periodic arrangement of the elements, the harmonic structure of crystals, the formal relationships evolved in the growth of living organisms. But creative freedom within that world of harmony—that is an individual achievement, the product of long exercise in aesthetic disciplines—poetry, dance, drama, the plastic arts. These disciplines should begin at the earliest age—in the nursery and the kindergarten—and should be the basic disciplines underlying every sphere of knowledge and education.

This, which is the substance of Plato's educational theory, was not advocated by Plato with the idea of creating more poets and artists—as we know, he did not believe in professional poets and banished them from his ideal republic. His aim was to create integrated personalities, human beings capable of good living—good citizens of the republic. The same theory was revived by Schiller, but it was not taken seriously: it certainly found no place in the development of the German educational system, though Herbart had some premonition of it. It had a place, however, in the romantic tradition, and it was a German, Friedrich Nietzsche, who more definitely than any other modern philosopher entered into the spirit of this essentially Hellenic conception of the moral value of aesthetic discipline.[3]

We cannot imagine UNESCO, or any national or international organization, committing itself to a pro-

---

[3] Cf. *Beyond Good and Evil*, s. 188.

gramme which would involve—let me be quite clear about it—the reform of all existing academic institutions, a complete break-away from a pedagogic tradition which had its origins in the Revival of Learning. Universities, academies, colleges, polytechnics, laboratories, institutes and gymnasia—even our day schools and kindergartens—represent vested interests of great antiquity and power. It would be easier to disband the armies and navies of the world than the forces which administer our educational systems. They must be left to die a natural death. The new institutions, the new methods of education, the inspired pedagogues who must precede a new civilization, will spring up piecemeal, in isolated and unexpected places. As a matter of fact it is in the Soviet Union, the country which has officially adopted a philosophy of dialectical materialism, that one of the most significant educational experiments of our time has taken place—I refer to the system of education developed by Makarenko in the colonies he organized for the *bisprizornie,* or vagabond children after the Revolution. Makarenko's methods were not specifically aesthetic, but he recognized that discipline was the end and not the means of education—its function not to regulate behaviour to a dead convention but to create a living social organism, a happy co-operative community. Discipline in this sense is but another word for *style,* and it was this imponderable quality which, in the land of dialectical materialism, emerged as the most necessary educative ideal: a style of living.

5. A MOLECULAR PROCESS

In general, the forms of action which alone are effective are personal, cellular, local, I would like to say *molecular*. In this connection I would bring to my support some words of Pestalozzi's which Jung once quoted:

> None of the institutions, measures, or means of education established for the masses and the need of men in the aggregate, whatever shape or form they may take, serve to advance human culture. In the vast majority of cases they are completely worthless for that purpose or directly opposed to it. Our race develops its human qualities in essence only from face to face, from heart to heart. It can do this only in small circles which gradually grow larger in the warmth of feeling and love, and in trust and confidence. All the means requisite for the education of man, to make him humane, to make him truly a man, are the concern of the individual and of such institutions as are closely and intimately attached to his heart and mind. They never have been, or never will be, the concern of civilization.[4]

[4] *Ideen* (Zurich, 1927), p. 187.

There is a further sentence or two of Pestalozzi's which bring together the two strands of my argument:

> The human race cannot maintain its social unity without some force which creates order. Law and art are forces of culture which unite men as individuals in independence and freedom. The forces at work in a cultureless civilization join men together in masses by the power of force alone, without taking into account independence, freedom, law, and art.

Independence, freedom, law and art—these are all implicit in aesthetic education, and it is only in so far as we oppose aesthetic education to scientific education, and to intellectual education in the tradition of the Renaissance, oppose it as a complete and adequate substitute for such bankrupt traditions, that any hope can be entertained for the future of our civilization. The renewal must be a moral renewal, springing up in the private life and family circles of humble people; it must be a product of their earliest education and a constant habit of their upbringing. The only habit that is ennobling, penetrating to the frame and physique as well as the soul of man, is the creative activity in all its rituals, exercises, festivities and practical services. What men do makes them what they are; *how* they do what they do determines the quality of what they are; and it is only when the doing is raised to the dignity of a regular or ritualistic art that it penetrates into the deepest recesses of the soul.

I hope I have not carried my argument on to a metaphysical plane which is outside the range of common discourse, but in any case I will end by being as concrete and specific as the subject allows. My argument is that any process of cultural revival or reconstruction must operate through the individual. *"Alles, was anfaengt, faengt stets im Kleinen an."* I take up the same position as Jung: "One goal is within our reach, and that is to develop and bring to maturity individual personalities." And just as Jung considers that the highest task of psychotherapy today is "to pursue with singleness of purpose the goal of the development of the individual," so I too consider that the person is the only ground in which a cultural renaissance can take place. "Renaissance," of course, is not a word we should use—it suggests a man awakening with a classical hangover. It is not a question of the rebirth of a tradition that has died: we are called upon to create a new tradition; not, perhaps, a transvaluation of all values, in Nietzsche's sense, but at least, in Nietzsche's sense, a forward-looking culture, a Dionysian instead of an Apollonian attitude to life.

The rebirth of a tragic sense of life; the re-emergence of transcendental forces so long frustrated by the lawless expansion of competitive instincts, by

crude materialism or by the elimination of human
sympathy from the processes of thought; the restora-
tion to life of significant play and ritual; a moral
healthiness which is affirmative, and not an inhibition
of all vitality; a sense of personal freedom and a
consequent responsibility for the endowment of one's
own fate with values; all these changes are involved as
groundwork for a new civilization. But it is unlikely
that these deep, subtle and intimate changes can be
brought about by secretariats and committees, by
international conferences and polyglot organizations.
They will be born in solitude, in meditation; in the
family circle and in the nursery school; in the field
and in the factory; in the face of specific problems
and by conscious discipline; in creative community
and in communal creations; in drama and in the
building of new cities; in dance and song; in moments
of mutual understanding and love. For all these moments and occasions, all that we need ask is peace in
our time and an end to the exploitation of man by
man.

But (and this is the bitter truth we must accept)
these intimate occasions are not created within an
artificial hegemony of nations. They are not a necessary consequence of the unity of nations: a unity of
nations can only be a consequence of them. So we
must begin with small things, in diverse ways, helping
one another, discovering one's own peace of mind,
waiting for the understanding that flashes from one

peaceful mind to another. In that way the separate cells will take shape, will be joined to one another, will manifest new forms of social organization and new types of art. From that multiplicity and diversity, that dynamic interplay and emulation, a new culture may arise, and mankind be united as never before in the consciousness of a common destiny.

VIII

ART AS A UNIFYING PRINCIPLE IN EDUCATION

1. INTERNATIONALISM

W E OFTEN CLAIM, with a certain pride, that the visual arts are an international language. Almost all international activities are concerned with the removal or dissolution of the barriers that separate nations, whether these are barriers of sovereignty, or barriers of custom and language, or merely barriers of trade. The visual arts know no such barriers, of time or of space. They constitute one language, and though this language has provincial accents, it is essentially a language of symbols that communicates a meaning without hindrance from country to country and across the centuries.

From this fact alone the visual arts in our time have acquired a new significance among nations that are more than ever conscious of the need for mutual understanding. The nations of the world have been brought nearer to each other by developments in the technical means of communication—air transport, wireless telephony, television—but the nearer they are drawn to each other by such physical means, the more poignantly they experience the remaining barrier of language.

There is, of course, a linguistic approach to this problem: the attempt to create an international language to be taught to the children of all countries. Such international languages have two disadvantages —they must be learned by rote and when so learned they remain artificial. They are not capable of expressing spontaneously the deepest intuitions and feelings of mankind. The visual arts do not suffer either of these limitations: they can be freely exchanged and fully appreciated among civilized peoples without any diminution of their authenticity. We must, however, examine their scope and possible applications before making unwarranted claims for their utility.

Let us first look a little more closely at the concept of internationalism. It is an ambiguous word. What, in the first place, is a nation? How does the concept differ from that of a race, a people, a society or a state? The ancient political philosophers Plato and Aristotle invariably spoke of the State—the State was the collective aspect of a people; and the principles of government, right down to the time of Rousseau, were never applied to amorphous entities of race or nation: they were formulated for voluntary associations of individual human beings, irrespective of race. The whole point of Rousseau's famous treatise was to demonstrate that the State is freely established by contract between politically conscious persons, and is not an entity arbitrarily determined by blood or geography, by despotism or destiny. The State is determined by a legal compact. "In the place of the individual personality of each contracting party," wrote Rousseau, "this act of association creates a moral and collective body, composed of as many members as the assembly contains votes, and receiving from this act its unity, its common identity, its life and its will." To continue with Rousseau's definition:

> This public person, so formed by the union of all other persons, formerly took the name of city and now takes the name of *Republic* or *body politic;* it is called by its members State when active, and *Power* when compared with others like itself. Those who are associated in it take collectively the name of *people,* and severally are called *citizens,* as sharing in the sovereign power, and *subjects,* as being under the laws of the State. But these terms are often confused and taken one for another . . . it is enough to know how to distinguish them when they are used with precision.[1]

---

[1] *The Social Contract,* trans. G. D. H. Cole (London, 1913), pp. 15–16.

It is far from my intention to discuss *The Social Contract* or Rousseau's conception of the State, but it will be seen that his comprehensive definitions do not include the word nation, and that is the significant point. The nation, and the concept of internationalism based on it, is an invention of the modern age.

As a matter of fact, Rousseau does use the word in the concluding sentences of his treatise, when he disclaims any intention of dealing with the State in its "external relations, which would include the law of nations, commerce, the right of war and conquest, public right, leagues, negotiations, treaties, etc." From this it would seem that the word came into use when it was necessary to distinguish one State from another as separate powers. That is to say, the nation was a legal concept, and its usage was probably established by those English jurists like Jeremy Bentham, John Austin and Sir Henry Maine who first began to discuss the international aspects of law a hundred years ago. The term international was apparently invented by Bentham, to describe what he called that branch of jurisprudence dealing with "the mutual transactions between sovereigns as such."[2]

---

[2] Introduction to the *Principles of Morals and Legislation* (1879), quoted from the Encyclopaedia Britannica, 11th ed., XIV (1910), p. 694.

2. UNIVERSALISM

I would now like, for the sake of my argument, to return to Rousseau's conception of the State as a voluntary association of freely acting persons, and to suggest that mutual transactions between persons (as distinct from States) require a name other than internationalism, which is based on the separatism and aggressiveness of nations. The obvious name is *universalism*. Internationalism is a legal or political concept; universalism a philosophical concept. As such it has an unduly restricted connotation, especially in medieval philosophy. But I use it as a term comprising the complete natural world, all particulars as well as all general notions or concepts. It is in this sense that Christianity, for example, claims to be a universal religion—we do not speak of an international church. Nor should we speak of international art when what we mean is a universal art.

What is universal is also natural, for nature is a general name for the particulars we observe in our universe, the universe of *things*. It was Rousseau's belief that our ideas are of universal validity only in so far as they are based on our direct perception of things, and that a natural education is one based on such perceptions. That is to say, a natural education is the progressive assimilation and co-ordination of the child's sense impressions, as he begins to explore the world of things around him. That is why Rousseau attached so much importance to the development of the child's curiosity. The order that the child introduces into his perceptions is aesthetic in its nature, being determined by an animal instinct for fitness or harmony. Rousseau always distinguished between the faculty of reasoning, which is a later development of the mind, and a moral sensibility based on the harmonious development of the senses. The case for education through art proceeds logically from this observation.

What we must now affirm, and deduce what consequences we may from the affirmation, is that the child's reactions to the universe of things are also universal, constant for the human race, natural to every child. There is not one way of reaction in an American child and another in a Chinese child, one way in a European child and another in an African child: the child's perceptual development is uniformly human. This I regard as perhaps the most significant fact established by our scientific observations of child art during the past fifty years. Whether we use the comparative method and assemble the evidence in international exhibitions of children's art, or use the analytical method and trace the mental development of the individual child, we are confronted with the same universal phenomenon—the use of a language of signs and symbols that is common to children of every race.

3. A UNIVERSAL LANGUAGE

Is it possible to regard this universal but neglected factor in human development as a basis for that "universal language" which Rousseau said must be created for mutual intercourse between all men? Rousseau asked for:

a kind of common organ of sensation *(sensorium commune)* that would perceive events wherever they occurred—that would be a tie binding all individuals together.[3]

But Rousseau did not perceive that such a tie might already exist, undeveloped, in the natural expression we give to our *sensorium commune,* namely, the plastic arts. He went on to elaborate the legal conception of such a tie, and so arrived at his ideal of a social contract, which would somehow (he was never quite clear *how*) unite all people in obedience to a universal law.

Rousseau's conception is philosophical, and based

---

[3] *Social Contract,* 1st draft, as quoted in *Political Writings of Jean Jacques Rousseau,* ed. C. E. Vaughan, vol. I (Cambridge, 1915), 449 f.

on nothing more concrete than the sentiment to which we give the name of conscience. Conscience, we may admit with Rousseau, is natural to man, older than all education, a simple gift of nature.[4]

But conscience remains a sentiment, a state of mind, until it is given *form,* and it is given form when it is reified—that is to say, when our feelings are organized and transmitted to others as affective artifacts. The discipline of art precedes and determines the discipline of conscience. That is the dogma first enunciated by Plato on which we must base a philosophy of education through art.

The development of the artistic activity in children, which when uninhibited is parallel to the development of perception in general, is at first a spontaneous reification of sensation. I use the word reification advisedly, to distinguish the process from expression in general, which may be internalized as thought, or made evident in ephemeral cries and gestures. What soon reveals itself in the child is a desire to perpetuate its feelings, to make a visual and sensible record of an invisible actuality. This is not yet the stage of representation, which is a conscious desire to indicate the appearance of the thing perceived rather than the sensation experienced in the act of perception. It is the stage of substitution, for which a symbol will suffice.

---

[4] Cf. Ernest Hunter Wright, *The Meaning of Rousseau* (Oxford, 1929), p. 14.

It has been shown by several investigators, but most effectively by Mrs. Rhoda Kellogg of San Francisco, that the expressive gestures of the infant, from the moment that they can be recorded by a crayon or pencil, evolve from certain basic scribbles towards consistent symbols. Over several years of development such basic patterns gradually become the conscious representation of objects perceived: the substitutive sign becomes a visual image. Scientists may object that the analysis of this process has not been carried far enough to justify a generalization, but we have an hypothesis that should hold the field until it has been proved to be false. According to this hypothesis every child, in its discovery of a mode of symbolization, follows the same graphic evolution. Out of the amorphous scribblings of the infant emerge first certain basic forms—the circle, the upright cross, the diagonal cross, the rectangle, etc.—and then two or more of these basic forms are combined into that comprehensive symbol known as the *mandala*, a circle divided into quarters by a cross. Let us ignore for the present the general psychological significance of the process: I merely want to draw attention to the fact that it is universal and is found, not only in the scribblings of children, but wherever the making of signs has had a symbolizing purpose—which is from the Neolithic Age onwards.

Mrs. Kellogg has shown that by slight degrees of modification the basic symbol, the mandala, can be a distinct substitute for many different objects. If the arms of the cross within the circle are extended beyond the circumference, the basic form becomes a symbol for the sun; extend the diameter laterally and add two lines to the base of the circle and it becomes a man; other modifications of the basic form stand for a house, a vehicle, a tree, and so on. The modifications of this basic form, the mandala, are capable of providing a language of symbols as extensive as the child's perceptual experience, and this language is universal.

At first such a language is geometrical and monochromatic, but the child is then provided with a variety of colours and these seem to be used indiscriminately. But colours, too, have their psychological significance, and in accordance with the child's emotional development, associations will be established between individual colours and particular experiences. Again I must pass by a lot of research in which an attempt has been made to sort out these correspondences—both on the level of simple association and at the deeper level of unconscious significance. In so far as these correspondences are perceptual, they may be determined by the colours prevailing in the child's environment, but some associations are of wider significance and may be made by children everywhere— red for fire, or anger, or the setting sun; blue for water or anything deep; yellow for flowers and the midday sun. It is only in so far as the individual child's emotional development has been subjected to unusual stress, or unusual deprivation, that colours take on an unusual or irrational significance.[5] In general the symbolism of colour is as universal as the symbolism of form.

4. A NATURAL LAW

So far I have been following the first seven or eight years of the child's life, before the nation or state has enlisted the child for purposes of its own. Up to that point education, in the hands of a successful teacher, has followed a line of development dictated by the child's own interest or desire. "Present interest," to quote Rousseau again, "that is the motive power, the only motive power that takes us far and safely." But now something other than present interest looms ahead—our educator calls it "life" or "reality," and by this he means obligations and distractions that conflict with the child's present interest—the manners and customs, the vocations and competition, of the society into which he and the child have been born. The principle of universality is then abandoned and in its place is substituted the tactics of social expedience. We use grand phrases to reconcile us to this process—the moulding of character, the training of

[5] Cf. "Colour Formations of the Unconscious Psyche," Jolande Jacobi, D. Phil., Palette, No. 12 (Basel, 1963).

the intellect, the discipline of the spirit. But all these phrases disguise the real nature of the process: for what is involved is the abandonment of present interest, the suppression or distortion of instinctive actions, the thwarting of natural tendencies. To quote Rousseau again:

> When our natural tendencies have not been interfered with by human prejudice and human institutions, the happiness alike of children and of men consists in the enjoyment of their liberty.

I shall be told that history has proved this to be a dangerous doctrine. But it depends on our reading of history and on our definition of liberty. The tragic consequences of the French Revolution, and of the greater social revolutions we have known in our own time, do not flow from the realization of Rousseau's doctrine—indeed all such revolutions have been a perversion of this doctrine, and have never for a moment entertained the true concept of liberty. The enjoyment of liberty remains our ideal, but we forget that only "that man is truly free who desires what he is able to perform, and does what he desires." This "fundamental maxim," as Rousseau called it, from which all his rules of education sprang, is the maxim we should now examine in the circumstances of our international conflicts.

Rousseau always sought to effect a correspondence

between action and environment. No contradiction should exist between environment and a fully functioning sensibility. Nature provides such an environment, but failing nature, that is to say, in an artificial society, the aim of education should be to reproduce natural conditions, so that the child's sensibility is free to develop "in contact with things only," that is to say, away from situations that involve a conflict between duty and desire.

Such moral realism is unknown today, for we accept such a conflict as inevitable and attempt to resolve it by authority. We accept the conflict between desire and duty as the natural condition of man, and our purpose is to control desire by the rule of law. It is true that the concept of a natural law does exist, even in jurisprudence, and to some extent what we call common law or custom is based on it. But we are now for the most part governed by statute law, and education itself has become a statutory system, established by acts of the legislature, administered by councils and committees, all directed to a purpose into which desire does not enter.

Against this statutory concept of education we may oppose an ideal that seeks freedom in necessity, the necessity of nature and natural law. The laws of organic growth, the laws of physics and the laws of cosmic evolution—these constitute a discipline that has no necessary correspondence to national statutory law—a discipline that is the inevitable condition of our existence. In obeying these laws we find our perfect freedom, which is also the perfect form towards which the human species evolves.

Most of these laws can be represented in symbolic form—geometrical structures, that reify numerical proportions in all possible dimensions. Man, in his long evolution, has gradually become conscious of these universal forms, and consciousness itself might be defined as an awareness of form. Mere sensation is not yet consciousness: but the ability to retain sensations as images, to compare and combine such images into meaningful structures—such is conscience, or consciousness. But we do not necessarily hold such structures in our consciousness: we take them into the evolving structure of the mind itself. They become the physically determined patterns of perception, and beyond our awareness control the habits of the mind. Such patterns of perception are called archetypes, and again they are universal.

As consciousness develops, these archetypes sink below the level of consciousness, where they exercise an unconscious control of our modes of imagination and thought. They are the patterns or moulds into which our feelings and fantasies automatically fit. What is archetypal is also universal, and civilizations in their evolution discover and repeat the same images, the same symbols and fantasies. These archetypes are not themselves phantasms: they are real things, built-in structures that give direction to our mental activities, and, more significantly for our present enquiry, give structure to our amorphous feelings. Such structured feelings we call works of art.

5. A VISUAL ORDER

The mechanism of the imagination is still a scientific mystery. The storing and classification of the myriad sensations that enter the brain; the stimulation and recall of these latent images; their spontaneous grouping into patterns of significance determined by a momentary premonition; the whole process of attention and will—psychology has little to say that is not speculative on these matters. But laws must exist in this realm as in all human behaviour that has a physical basis.

Our policy of education through art is based on the hypothesis that the images we evoke in the course of any kind of cognitive activity have a universal significance, and correspond to something permanent and unchanging in the nature of man. If this hypothesis is true, then the pursuit of these images is an enterprise common to all mankind. All mankind is united by natural propensity in the desire and pursuit of universal images or archetypes, those forms which Plato identified with Truth.

Plato's forms are metaphysical, though there are curious passages in his works in which he suggests

that his archetypal ideas have a geometrical structure.
The famous passage from *Philebus*[6] is too well known
to quote, but much as it has mystified later philosophers, it is an intuition of the formal nature of the
archetypes. The mind, in its effort to arise from the
amorphous pool of sensation and feeling, clings to a
scaffold of precise geometric figures. Nowhere is this
more clearly demonstrated than in the slow but certain emergence of basic forms from the apparently
aimless scribbling activity of a child. Form, the basic
pattern, precedes identity, precedes significance, controls imagination, determines intelligence. The archetypes are the structural elements of visual order,
of cognition itself, and the archetypes are by definition universal.

Visual order—let us consider for a moment the
significance of this apparently insignificant phrase. In
relation to individual development it is the preliminary
to rational apprehension itself: if we do not construe
our visual sensation in an order, we are momentarily
confused or, if the disorder persists, mindless or mad.
The various forms of schizophrenia are due to such
perceptual disorder. But if we pass from the individual
to the public person, to mankind in its collective
aspect, then it would be no mere analogy to assert
that visual order is the mark or characteristic of a
civilization. From the first settlements in the Neolith-

---

[6] *Philebus,* 51 b, c.

ic Age to the great civilizations of Egypt, Assyria, Greece and Rome, what distinguishes such collective entities is a visual order, represented in their buildings, their schemes of irrigation, their cultivated fields, their alphabets and visual signs; and such civilizations advance in the degree that they refine the first elementary order introduced into their shelters, their tools and weapons, their primitive signs. Civilization might be defined as the achievement of visual order— I can conceive of no more significant definition.

Then let us observe that just as a visual order develops in the individual by virtue of certain elementary archetypal forms, so a civilization develops by virtue of the combination and refinement of the same basic visual forms. The history of Greek architecture, for example, can be interpreted as the gradual refinement of the proportions of elementary geometrical figures such as the square, the rectangle, the triangle, the cone and the cylinder, and of these figures in combination. The decoration that was added to·these structures had no structural significance. Sculpture, in so far as it is not to be identified with architecture, is an art with its own distinct process of visual refinement.

The same process of visual ordering takes place in all the great architectural styles, the differences being determined by the priority given to particular geometrical figures. The only fundamental difference between the classical and the Gothic order is the difference between the architrave and the vault, between rectangular and curved solutions of the same problems. Refinement, that is to say, is within limits an arbitrary process and leaves room for the play of human sensibility (itself a variation due to varieties of climate and skill). But the desire to achieve visual order is a universal desire, and the process of achievement has been repeated in every localized civilization. What we now desire is a universal visual order to correspond with a universal civilization. How can this be achieved?

Only, of course, by a process of refinement that begins with archetypal forms and bases upon these a universal visual order, a universal art and a universal civilization. It may be that this process can be initiated only by universal desire—that a universal will must precede the invention of such a process of visual ordering. But surely such a will exists in the mind of man. I do not discount the existence of contrary impulses—the impulse to self-destruction, the death-wish diagnosed by Freud. But Freud also posited a counter force, the libido, the life-wish, and we may suppose that all our endeavours are subject to this fundamental dialectic of existence—an idea not unfamiliar to the ancient philosophers. But what we call civilization, the amelioration of our brute existence, is built on the erotic impulse, the desire to live and to propagate our kind. It is this impulse that we educate through art, and our whole philosophy of education through art is a salutation to Eros, a recognition of the fact that the only challenge to death is an eternal affirmation of the creative will of man.

6. *A SALUTATION TO EROS*

The creative will of man is also the will to love one another, for we create a visual order not for our own delight, but to communicate our feelings to one another. That is why we may call our philosophy of education through art a salutation to Eros. Here I might repeat some words used by James Baldwin in his "Letter from a Region in my Mind":

> Love takes off the masks that we fear and cannot live within. I use the word "love" here not merely in the personal sense but as a state of being, or a state of grace—not in the infantile American sense of being made happy but in the tough and universal sense of quest and daring and growth.[7]

That is the sense in which I, too, use the word love. The will to love, the will to live, the will to create and communicate our true feelings to other men—these are all aspects of Eros and the only solvent for the racial hatreds that now torment our existence.

I assume, therefore, that a will to live should and

---

[7] *The Fire Next Time* (London, 1963), pp. 102–3.

does prevail; moreover, that this will is expressed as an instinct for order. But I also recognize—we must all recognize—the existence of what has been called "the animal sources of our nature," the fact that "man is a predator with an instinct to kill," which is merely another aspect, the evolutionary aspect, of the death-wish. If the death-wish is expressed in the evolution of weapons of destruction, the life-wish is represented by the gradual refinement of these weapons until they lose their destructive function and become works of art, ritual objects removed from slaughter and death and dedicated to life and resurrection. Weapons no less than tools and dwellings and all things that man has learned to make are subject to the law of refinement, the instinct for order.[8] Which is another way of saying that the imagination seeks and finds archetypal forms. Civilization is the search for these forms; civilizations decline when they relinquish the creation of form. "Civilization," writes an anthropologist who claims to be a realist, an anti-romantic, "is a product of evolution and an expression of nature's most ancient law. Far antedating the predatory urge in our animal nature, far more deeply buried than conscience or territory or society lies that shadowy, mysterious, undefinable command of the kind, the instinct for order."[9]

---

[8] Cf. Herbert Read, *The Origins of Form in Art* (London and New York, 1965), pp. 66–88.

[9] Robert Ardrey, *African Genesis* (London, 1961), p. 352.

This anthropologist, Robert Ardrey, believes in
original sin, or the basic ugliness of human nature.
So do I, but I also believe in original beauty, which
is the antidote to sin or ugliness. I believe in original
beauty, which is the constructive use of the libido, the
life-wish. Art is a domestication of the instincts. "Art,
and art only," said Tolstoy, "can cause violence to
be set aside." That is why I have called art a process
of refinement, but it is a practical process, a skill,
measuring the crude forces of instinct against the
archetypal forms. We control the instincts, even the
predatory instincts, by giving them form. The forms
are universal, beyond the predatory individual, beyond
the warring nation: the forms of universal art. To
superimpose the instinct for order on the predatory
instincts—such is the purpose of education, more particularly of education through art. The order is universal—art is one: a universal education through art
is the basis for a universal order in society, a universal
civilization. I see no other basis, for order is a physical
thing, a structure built into our instinctual life, and
that order, as it takes shape in our moral sensibility,
is aesthetic, is art. A universal art is therefore the
surest and perhaps the only basis that an everlasting
peace can seek and maintain.

These considerations are general and philosophic,
and may seem far removed from the mundane activities of the school and college. But it is my conviction that the policy of education through art is of

vital significance in the present world situation, and that we cannot confront that situation with anything less than a philosophy of education that is at the same time a philosophy of life. I believe that we possess in the principles of art, which are the principles of a creative activity, an antidote to the forces of destruction that now threaten the existence of the human race. Unless we can succeed in basing education on the natural instinct for order, education will remain powerless against the forces of destruction. The instinct for order is the only natural instinct that can control the instinct for destruction, the mortal instinct. Art is the name that we give to the only human activity that can establish a universal order in all we do and make, in thought and in imagination. Education through art is education for peace.